AI Simplified

Harnessing Microsoft Technologies for Cost-Effective Artificial Intelligence Solutions

D1526337

Empower Your Existing Team to Build Low-Cost, Low-Risk, Highly-Functional AI Applications with Microsoft Tools They Already Know

Disclaimer

This material is for informational purposes and does not constitute medical, legal, financial, or other actionable advice.

The author and publisher disclaim any liability for any losses or damages resulting from the use of the information contained in this book, including but not limited to business losses, technical issues, or inaccuracies. The information is provided "as is" and without warranties of any kind, either express or implied. Readers should seek appropriate professional advice for their specific circumstances.

Any references to third-party companies, products, or services are for informational purposes only and do not imply endorsement or affiliation unless expressly stated.

The author and publisher make no guarantees as to the completeness, accuracy, or timeliness of the information provided. Readers are encouraged to verify information with other sources.

Table of Contents

Dedication

T o my friends and family, who are the strong roots of my journey. Like a majestic tree, your guidance and support have provided the foundation from which I've grown. Your belief in me has kept me grounded, steady, and ever reaching higher.

And to those who doubted, underestimated, or wronged me—you were the storms that battered the tree, making its trunk stronger and its branches stretch even further. You gave me the drive, the fire, and the motivation to push harder, think bigger, and prove you wrong. You were the fuel that kept me going.

Prologue

As an engineer, I see myself first and foremost as a scientist. My work is guided by the principles of the scientific method: observation, hypothesis, experimentation, and analysis. This book represents my hypotheses on the intersection of AI, business, programming, databases, and the broader executive and management landscapes. It's an exploration of how these domains come together to drive innovation and efficiency.

In presenting these ideas, I recognize that no single viewpoint or hypothesis fits every situation. I encourage you, the reader, to engage with these concepts critically. When are the statements made in this book true? Under what circumstances—whether assumptions, industries, or departments—do they hold up? And equally important, when do they not? Why might they fall short, and how can they be adjusted to better reflect different contexts?

This book is intended to start a conversation. With feedback and analysis from those involved in all of these affected communities, we can refine these ideas and improve how AI is applied in business. Your insights will be invaluable for the evolution of these hypotheses and for future editions.

I welcome your feedback at:

KeithBaldwin@AInDotNet.com

Together, through analysis and collaboration, we can advance the effective integration of AI in business and achieve better outcomes for   everyone.

Introduction

"The journey of a thousand miles begins with one step."

- Lao Tzu

Welcome to the exciting world of Artificial Intelligence (AI)—a key player in today's technological revolution! This book is your guide to understanding how AI can transform the way businesses operate, enhancing efficiency and opening up new opportunities across diverse industries.

AI has evolved from a lofty sci-fi dream to a robust toolkit that's redefining decision-making, customer interactions, and operational processes in real time. Whether your goal is to streamline workflows, improve customer satisfaction, or drive innovation, AI has a pivotal role to play.

Our aim is to demystify AI for business leaders, managers, and professionals like you who are eager to tap into its capabilities within your own organizations. We will cover the essentials of AI, its wide-ranging applications, and the practical steps needed to craft and deploy AI solutions. By the time you turn the final page, you will possess the insights and knowledge necessary to integrate AI into your business and maintain a competitive edge in our dynamic economic environment.

As we venture into this transformative journey, take full advantage of the resources this book offers—packed with case studies, real-life examples, and a thorough breakdown of AI tools and technologies. Let's embark on this path together and chart a course toward a smarter, more efficient business future.

Purpose of the Book

The main goal of this book is to equip business leaders, executives, managers, programmers, and database administrators with the knowledge and tools they need to effectively leverage Artificial Intelligence (AI) within their organizations. Our mission is to make AI approachable and actionable for businesses eager to exploit this potential.

AI can appear overwhelming, shrouded in jargon and complex technicalities. Yet, when demystified and implemented effectively, it can address critical business challenges, automate mundane tasks, perform functions beyond the scope of traditional programming, and provide insights that inform strategic decisions. This book offers a straightforward, practical guide to applying AI in business settings, focusing on real-world applications over the intricacies of algorithms or coding.

Another purpose of this book is to establish a baseline and roadmap for everyone in your organization: executives, managers, stakeholders, developers, and database administrators. We provide a practical, iterative roadmap for innovating with AI and computer software. By following this roadmap, your organization will align on a unified approach to AI development, starting with prototypes, moving to minimally viable products (MVPs), and ultimately achieving production-ready systems. This approach emphasizes quick iteration and learning, allowing your team to adapt and refine the process to suit your specific needs while ensuring that everyone is moving in the same direction.

By the end of your journey through this book, you should be able to:

- Grasp the essential concepts and terminology of AI

- Recognize AI's transformative potential across various business operations

- Formulate an effective AI Innovation Team

- Spot opportunities for integrating AI solutions into your daily processes

- Navigate the plethora of AI tools and technologies with a special emphasis on Microsoft platforms

- Craft a strategic plan for AI adoption that aligns with your business goals and ethical standards

Whether you're just starting to explore AI or seeking to expand your existing knowledge and application of the technology, this book is designed to be an invaluable guide as you transition toward an AI-driven business model.

About the Book Series

This book is the beginning of a series designed to equip businesses with the practical know-how to apply artificial intelligence (AI) effectively. As the inaugural book, our aim is to lay a non-technical foundation, offering a broad perspective on integrating AI into business operations—a crucial first step for those ready to embrace this technology.

In subsequent books, we'll delve into "quick wins"—AI tools that businesses can implement swiftly to see immediate benefits. These tools are designed to allow you to start experimenting with AI, enhancing your understanding through hands-on experience and observable results.

Our series is not about designing new AI technologies; instead, it's about teaching you how to use existing AI tools effectively, akin to learning how to drive a car without needing to engineer its components. We advocate starting with simple applications before moving on to more complex and costly options. Often, the most straightforward approach can address your needs without the expense and complexity pushed by big cloud providers.

Each book in the series will address the following key aspects:

1. Understanding the AI technology relevant to your business

The AI applications we promote are just like other business applications you have running in your business

2. Exploring the capabilities of the AI technology

3. Examining practical use cases

4. Assessing the business benefits and problem-solving potential of specific AI tools

5. Comparing these tools with other market options

6. Implementing these tools in a straightforward, cost-effective, and low-risk manner

7. Discussing various implementation approaches including low-code/no-code options like Microsoft CoPilot and Power Platform, the more hands-on Visual Studio method, and the comprehensive but higher barrier-to-entry Azure

8. Also, exploring other platforms such as AWS and Google AI when Microsoft solutions don't fully meet your needs

Our goal for each book is to provide you with actionable knowledge and free, real-working C# and VB.NET code prototypes for common AI applications. These prototypes are designed to be up and running quickly, allowing your developers to scale them into fully operational systems.

As you progress through the series, starting with the second book, you will read the book, download code, build prototypes, and demonstrate these to your stakeholders and customers. This hands-on experience is invaluable as it fosters learning and adaptation within your business environment.

For those who require more robust solutions, we offer enhanced versions of each application for purchase, featuring additional functionalities. This approach ensures that we can continue to provide extensive resources while also sustaining our efforts.

You can hire us to help develop applications and services if you don't have developers, your developers are too busy, or your company or development team wants some consulting, training, or support.

> **"Technology, through automation and artificial intelligence, is definitely one of the most disruptive sources."**
>
> **Alain Dehaze**

By the end of this series, you should have a suite of AI applications at your disposal, integrating AI seamlessly into your business operations without the daunting price tags often associated with big cloud solutions. This series promises a journey from foundational knowledge to advanced implementation, all tailored to empower your business in the AI landscape.

Target Audience

This book is crafted for a diverse audience of business leaders, executives, managers, programmers, database administrators, and professionals eager to explore and implement Artificial Intelligence (AI) within their organizations. It's an essential resource for anyone from the upper echelons of corporate leadership to those managing day-to-day operations across various sectors.

Our target audience includes:

- Business Leaders and Executives: CEOs, CTOs, CIOs, and other senior executives aiming to harness AI to foster innovation, streamline operations, and secure a competitive advantage.

- Managers and Team Leaders: From middle managers to project leaders, this book provides insights into how AI can be tailored to enhance specific business areas and how to spearhead AI-driven projects effectively.

- Business Professionals: Business analysts, consultants, and strategists looking to integrate AI into their decision-making and business models will find this book particularly useful.

- Stakeholders and Subject Matter Experts (SMEs): Those responsible for overseeing business processes will gain a better understanding of AI's potential impacts on their operations and how it can be integrated seamlessly into existing workflows.

- Entrepreneurs and Innovators: Startup founders and innovative thinkers exploring AI as a means to disrupt traditional markets and create novel opportunities will find valuable guidance.

- Programmers and Database Administrators: Technical professionals who will execute the AI implementations are provided with practical applications and prototype code to transform theory into practice.

This book does not require readers to have prior technical knowledge of AI or computer science. Instead, it offers a straightforward, comprehensible introduction to AI's practical business applications, empowering readers to make well-informed decisions about adopting AI technologies in their organizations.

The Problem We Solve

The prevailing approach within large cloud platforms like Azure, AWS, and Google often suggests that developing AI applications requires a complete overhaul of your existing development

> **"Innovation distinguishes between a leader and a follower."**
>
> **Steve Jobs**

framework. They advocate hiring entirely new teams with specialized titles, doling out hefty salaries, and committing to steep ongoing expenses in AI services. Not to mention the steep learning curve associated with new programming languages, development tools, platforms, DevOps, and logging systems. This traditional route can lead to investing millions of dollars and years of development with a startling 80 percent risk of failure.

Is it worth spending $500,000 and potentially wasting years to develop a mere prototype with such high risks?

Consider a more pragmatic approach—investing in your existing .NET development team by providing them with resources like our books, which come with working prototype code. This method significantly reduces your risk and cost.

With our book, a developer can quickly read through, download the provided code, and have a working prototype running in just a few days. You can then demonstrate this prototype to your stakeholders and Subject Matter Experts (SMEs), gather their feedback, refine the prototype based on their insights, and iterate again. This iterative process dramatically accelerates development and reduces both costs and risks.

Additionally, big cloud consultants often require you to define all requirements upfront, and change orders are very expensive. In contrast, we promote an agile approach where you start with a few requirements and define more requirements as you iterate and learn. This flexibility allows for adjustments based on real-world feedback and evolving needs, making the development process more adaptive and cost-effective.

Choosing the Right Approach for Your Business

We recognize that one approach doesn't fit all when it comes to AI adoption. Depending on your resources, existing infrastructure, and strategic goals, different approaches might suit your needs better. Here's a breakdown of the paths you could take:

> **Never leave AI unmonitored. Always record, request, response, real human review (if less than perfect), and human notes (optional: what did they actually get versus what they expected).**

Low Cost, No Development – Internet-Based AI Tools

If you are a solopreneur or have only a few employees, if budget constraints limit your ability to hire developers, or if you prefer not to engage in development—Internet-based AI tools are a practical choice. Our website resources (AInDotNet.com) provide directories and a selection of common AI tools that are quick to deploy with either monthly or annual fees. If you opt for these services:

1. This book remains a valuable resource packed with relevant insights.

2. For deeper dives into each tool, our subsequent books can guide you.

3. Explore the directories and top AI services listed in our website resources (www.AInDotNet.com). These can serve as benchmarks for the types of services you can develop using our approach described in future books.

Low Code/No Code Development

For those not professionally trained in programming but familiar with Microsoft software, Microsoft's Power Platform and CoPilot are excellent starting points. These tools are particularly useful for:

1. Individuals with some coding experience in environments like Microsoft Excel or Access. While these tools simplify programming, they have their limits and may eventually require traditional coding to meet complex needs.

2. Professional .NET programmers should explore these tools to learn AI concepts. However, consider the limitations of low code / no code tools in terms of complexity and scalability and the potential lack of support for advanced development practices like functionality, source control, versioning, and DevOps.

.NET Framework AI Tools

We advocate for the .NET framework as a robust solution for business AI application development, offering excellent cost-to-performance benefits:

- .NET and Visual Studio support a variety of programming languages and provide a powerful environment to develop any application type.

- If you're a .NET developer or manage a team of .NET developers, our books will provide the necessary knowledge to transition smoothly into AI development.

- The .NET framework allows you to build most any type of application (console, desktop, mobile, web, API, etc.), whereas the other options are limited.

Apple or Google Software Users

For businesses primarily using Apple or Google software, our .NET-based approach might not be the best fit. While .NET applications can run on Apple and Linux systems, it may not be the most efficient path for your needs. However, the foundational AI knowledge in our books is still valuable across different platforms.

Azure, AWS, Google Platforms

For highly complex projects like developing deep learning and neural network applications that demand significant resources, the specialized infrastructure and expertise offered by big cloud providers might be the best choice.

> Instead of changing your business processes to work with an AI application, you can write custom AI applications that conform to your business processes, giving you a competitive advantage.

For the majority of AI applications:

- .NET can suffice in most business AI applications, and where it falls short, cloud-based AI services that perform well and are reasonably priced can be integrated via APIs.

- Consider cloud services for specific needs, like OCR, where cloud services outperform available .NET libraries.

We respect the roles of AI engineers, ML engineers, and data scientists in designing large-scale, complex AI systems. However, for the application of AI, these specialists are usually not required. Like database administrators, their expertise is invaluable in complex scenarios, but for general AI application needs, a well-rounded .NET development approach can effectively meet business requirements.

Overview of Resources Offered

To support your journey in applying AI to your business, we offer a variety of resources designed to provide further insights, guidance, and practical tools. Here's an overview of what you can expect:

Free Social Media: Follow us on Twitter and LinkedIn for regular updates, tips, and discussions on the latest trends in AI and business.

Free Website: Our website serves as a hub for all our resources, including articles, blog posts, news, and access to our other platforms.

Free Newsletter: Subscribe to our newsletter for curated content, industry news, and exclusive insights delivered directly to your inbox. We give away free cheat sheets, whitepapers, guides, and other valuable resources.

Low Cost Books: In addition to this book, we offer other books that delve deeper into specific aspects of AI and its application in various business contexts. There are sometimes free resources for each book.

Free C# or VB.NET Prototype Code: With most books, we provide free C# or VB.NET prototype code for some of the most popular AI applications, allowing you to quickly, easily, for a low cost experiment and explore the potential of that AI topic for your business.

Enhanced AI Applications: For businesses looking for more advanced solutions, we sell enhanced AI applications tailored to specific industry needs and challenges.

Coaching, Consulting, and Training: Our team is available for personalized coaching, consulting, and training services to help you develop and implement AI strategies that align with your business goals.

Custom AI Application Development: We can work with you to develop custom AI applications and services that meet your needs. Please contact us with your requirements.

These resources are designed to complement the content of this book and provide you with ongoing support as you navigate the world of AI in business. Whether you're looking for inspiration, practical tools, or expert guidance, we're here to help you succeed in your AI journey.

For more information:

https://AInDotNet.com

KeithBaldwin@AInDotNet.com

Gartner, and others, estimate that up to 80% of AI projects will fail

https://www.forbes.com/sites/cognitiveworld/2022/08/14/the-one-practice-that-is-separating-the-ai-successes-from-the-failures/

https://www.techrepublic.com/article/why-85-of-ai-projects-fail/

https://hbr.org/2023/11/keep-your-ai-projects-on-track

We feel a lot of AI projects fail because a lot of companies get AI people and try to teach them the development of production-ready applications instead of taking development people and teaching them AI.

We think the best AI developers are .NET developers with 10, 15, 20 years of development experience. They know how to develop business applications. They know how to deliver working applications. They know the difference between prototypes and production code. They know source control, DevOps, testing, and security.

To be the best AI application developers, all they need is a little knowledge. We provide that knowledge.

Part 1:
Understanding AI

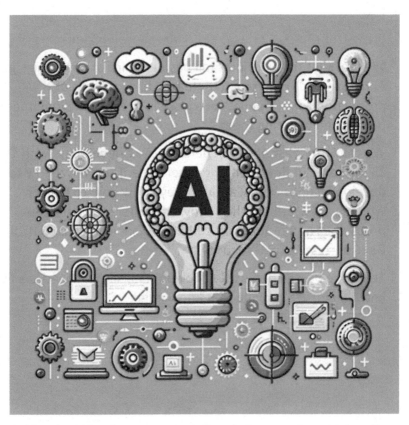

"*Machine learning is a core, transformative way by which we're rethinking how we're doing everything.*"

– Jeff Dean, Senior Fellow at Google, in an interview with *The Verge* (2018).

Chapter 1:
The AI Revolution

The march of progress and innovation is a fundamental aspect of human history, driven by our innate curiosity and desire to improve our circumstances. Attempts to halt this forward momentum are not only futile but often counterproductive, as they can stifle the very advancements that solve our most pressing challenges. Throughout history, each wave of technological innovation—from the industrial revolution to the digital age—has reshaped society, economies, and the global landscape, often for the better.

Today, artificial intelligence (AI) represents the next frontier in this continual progression. AI stands poised to redefine the boundaries of possibility, offering unprecedented opportunities for growth, efficiency, and problem-solving. Like electricity or the Internet, AI is becoming a transformative force across all sectors, driving innovations that were once the realm of science fiction.

Embracing AI is not merely about keeping up with technological trends; it is about actively participating in the shaping of our future, leveraging the tools of today to build a better tomorrow. We cannot stop innovation; the best we can do is strive to understand it and the profound changes it has instigated over thousands of years.

In this chapter, we embark on a journey through the history and evolution of technological innovations. From the earliest tools crafted by our ancestors to the sophisticated artificial intelligence systems of today, we'll explore the pivotal moments and breakthroughs that have shaped our world. Understanding this historical context will provide a foundation for understanding the transformative potential of AI in the modern era.

History and Evolution of Technological Innovations

The journey of technological innovation is a captivating narrative of human creativity and the relentless drive for advancement. From the primal discovery of fire to the cutting-edge development of artificial intelligence, each innovation has profoundly reshaped our world and our daily lives. This chapter delves into the history and evolution of technological innovations, spotlighting key milestones that have set the stage for the rise of artificial intelligence.

The Dawn of Technology

Technology's saga began with the development of early human inventions, such as the wheel and the lever, which fundamentally changed transportation and construction. The creation of writing systems and the printing press revolutionized communication, allowing knowledge to be preserved and disseminated across continents and epochs.

> **Historical Evolution**
>
> Technological innovations have evolved from simple tools and machines to complex systems, with key milestones such as the industrial revolution, the discovery of electricity, and the digital revolution shaping our world

The Industrial Revolution

A pivotal era, the industrial revolution brought mechanization and steam power, leading to mass production and the advent of factories. Innovations like the steam engine, the locomotive, and the telegraph catalyzed rapid industrialization and enhanced global connectivity.

The Age of Electricity

The harnessing of electricity triggered another surge of innovation, giving us the light bulb, the telephone, and the electric motor. Electricity transformed industries and daily life, infusing homes and businesses with new conveniences and linking the world more closely than ever before.

The Digital Revolution

The mid-20th century marked the beginning of the digital revolution, spearheaded by the invention of the transistor and the proliferation of computers. The birth of the Internet and the World Wide Web revolutionized communication, commerce, and information access, heralding the information age.

The Era of Artificial Intelligence

While the concept of artificial intelligence originated in the mid-20th century, it was the monumental advances in computing power and data accessibility that thrust AI to the forefront of technology. Today, AI is transforming multiple sectors, including health care, finance, transportation, and entertainment, by enhancing data analysis, automation, and decision-making processes.

Do Not Believe AI!

When computers first came out, some people believed everything a computer told them. We had to instruct computer users: "Don't believe everything a computer tells you!"

When the Internet first came out, some people believed everything they read on the Internet. I assume you've heard the saying "Don't believe everything you read on the Internet"?

Now, with AI, some people believe everything AI tells them. No. Stop.

AI Large Language Models are known to hallucinate (just make up random information, even facts). Independently verify everything AI says. Does it make sense? If it does not make sense, dig into it deeper. With some AI tools, you can ask follow-up questions such as "Where did you research that?", "What sources do you have?" Better yet—do a separate Google search to confirm the data.

Conclusion

The history of technological innovation stands as a testament to human ingenuity and our perpetual quest for progress. As we stand on the cusp of the AI revolution, understanding the path that led us here is crucial. This journey not only illuminates the transformative impact of technology on society—transitioning us from nomadic lifestyles to urban and suburban living—but also helps us appreciate AI's potential to shape our future further. In the next chapter, we will explore the implications of the AI revolution, examining how it will influence businesses and society at large.

Each technological leap has not only redefined society but also reshaped the job landscape, phasing out old roles and forging new ones, thus continually transforming our social structures and how we interact with the world around us.

Impact of AI on Society

The impact of Artificial Intelligence (AI) on society is profound and multifaceted, touching various aspects of our daily lives and the broader world. The following list digs into just some of these aspects:

Economic Growth: AI has the potential to significantly drive economic growth by enhancing productivity, optimizing supply chains, and fostering innovation. It can also spur the creation of new markets and industries centered around AI technologies, reshaping the economic landscape.

Employment: While AI is set to automate certain jobs, it simultaneously creates new opportunities for roles that require expertise in AI development, maintenance, and ethical oversight. This shift may necessitate workforce retraining and education to equip individuals with the skills needed to thrive in an evolving job landscape.

Health care: AI is transforming health care by improving diagnostic accuracy, personalizing treatment plans, expediting the design of new drugs, enabling remote robotic surgery, and enhancing patient care through predictive analytics and intelligent medical devices. These advancements promise to increase the efficiency and effectiveness of health services.

Ethics and Privacy: The adoption of AI introduces significant ethical and privacy concerns, especially regarding data usage, surveillance, and the autonomy of decision-making processes. To mitigate these risks and protect individual rights, it is imperative to foster responsible and transparent AI development practices.

Social Interaction: AI technologies, such as chatbots, virtual assistants, and social robots, are redefining human interaction with technology and each other. While these tools offer unprecedented convenience, they also provoke important questions about the nature of human connections and the appropriate role of machines in social contexts.

In conclusion, AI is reshaping society in numerous important ways, presenting a wide range of opportunities and challenges. As we delve deeper into AI's capabilities, it becomes increasingly crucial to consider its ethical dimensions and aim for a balanced approach that optimizes benefits while minimizing potential harms. This ensures that AI contributes positively to societal progress and helps build a future where technology enhances human well-being.

What a graphics designer developed because Dall-E was horrible in 2023

What Dall E generated in 2024. It's impressive but does not convey like the image from the graphic designer.

In the late 19th century, the world witnessed the dawn of the automobile era, but not everyone was ready to embrace this newfangled contraption. Enter the "Red Flag Laws," a curious chapter in the history of the United Kingdom and the United States, where fears and skepticism shrouded the potential of these mechanical marvels.

In the heart of the UK, the Locomotive Act of 1865, famously dubbed the "Red Flag Act," imposed a peculiar sight on the streets: a trio guiding an automobile, with one individual, flag in hand, marching 60 yards ahead to alert horse riders and carriage drivers of the impending mechanical beast. The message was clear: caution, innovation crossing!

Across the pond, Vermont, USA, echoed this cautious sentiment in 1894.

These laws, products of their time, reveal the trepidation societies face when confronting disruptive technologies. They stand as a testament to the human instinct to tread carefully into the unknown, to protect the familiar from the unforeseen.

Fast forward to today, and we find ourselves at a similar crossroads with Artificial Intelligence (AI). The same mix of awe and anxiety that once surrounded automobiles now envelopes AI. Should we, in a modern twist, have someone wave a red flag in offices where AI is at work?

The Red Flag Laws remind us that innovation often arrives hand in hand with fear. Yet, history shows us that understanding, adaptation, and regulation can transform apprehension into progress. As we navigate the AI landscape, let's ponder: what lessons can we draw from our ancestors' cautious waltz with automobiles? How can we ensure that our journey with AI is a safe advancement?

What a graphic designer developed in 2023 because Dall-E was horrible.

What Dall-E generated in 2024. This image
conveys the concepts we want.

Chapter 2:
What is AI?

In this chapter, we demystify key concepts and terminology, address common misconceptions, and shed light on the practical applications of AI across various industries. By understanding the nuances of AI and its real-world implications, we can better appreciate its potential to drive innovation and create value in the modern era.

We're going to introduce a lot of AI terminology in this chapter. If you're planning to work with AI, learning the jargon is a necessary step.

However, don't feel pressured to memorize all the terms right away—this chapter is designed to be a reference. Skim through it now and come back to it whenever needed. Each time you revisit, you'll absorb a little more.

Defining Artificial Intelligence

There is no singular definition of AI, as its interpretation varies widely depending on specific use cases and perspectives. For instance, theoretical AI researchers view AI through a different lens compared to applied AI researchers like ourselves. In light of this, we will provide multiple definitions and frameworks tailored to suit the diverse contexts in which you might discuss AI. This approach will equip you with the flexibility to adapt your understanding and communication according to your audience.

> Ask 10 AI experts to define AI and you're likely to get 15 answers. There is no one universal answer.

One definition of Artificial Intelligence (AI) is the simulation of human intelligence processes by machines, especially computer systems. These processes include the ability to reason, discover meaning, generalize, or learn from past experiences. AI is built on the foundation of algorithms and computational models that enable machines to carry out tasks that typically require human intelligence, such as recognizing patterns, making decisions, and solving problems.

Traditional computer programs operate under a deterministic framework: If conditions A and B are true, then X equals 10. In contrast, AI approaches problems probabilistically. It might determine actions based on the highest probability; for instance, if A is most likely true in Category 1 and B is most likely true in Category 2, then let X equal 10.

A Classic Definition of AI

Artificial intelligence (AI), machine learning (ML), deep learning, and generative AI are terms often mistakenly used interchangeably. While there can be some overlap, each usually represents a distinct concept within the broader field of AI, and understanding the nuances between them is key to fully grasping the scope of AI technologies.

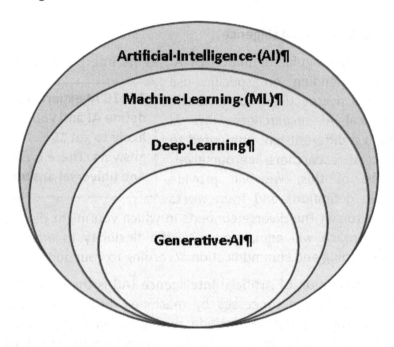

Artificial Intelligence (AI)

AI is the broadest category, encompassing any technique that enables machines to mimic human-like intelligence. This includes capabilities like problem-solving, decision-making, and learning. AI can be rule-based, relying on predefined rules for decision-making, or it can be adaptive, learning from data, which leads into the realm of machine learning.

Here are several key types of problems that AI is commonly used to solve:

1. Automation of Routine Tasks: AI excels at automating repetitive and routine tasks, such as data entry, transaction processing, and basic customer service inquiries through chatbots and virtual assistants. This not only increases efficiency but also allows human workers to focus on more complex and creative tasks.

2. Complex Decision-making: AI systems, especially those integrated with machine learning, can analyze large volumes of data to make informed decisions. This is particularly useful in areas like financial services for credit scoring, investment decisions, and fraud detection.

3. Healthcare Diagnostics and Treatment: AI algorithms help diagnose diseases from medical images, predict patient risks, and personalize treatment plans. Systems can detect nuances in data at speeds and accuracies that surpass human capabilities, such as identifying cancerous tissues in radiology images.

4. Enhancing Customer Experiences: AI recommends products to users based on their browsing and purchase history (e-commerce recommendations) and personalizes social media or streaming content feeds.

5. Speech Recognition and Natural Language Processing (NLP): AI powers voice-activated assistants, real-time translation apps, and other tools that can understand and generate human language. This technology is used in customer service, automated transcription services, and interactive educational tools.

> **Types of AI**
>
> **AI can be categorized into narrow AI (specific tasks) and general AI (replicating human cognitive abilities), with the former being more prevalent in current applications.**

6. Computer Vision: AI enables machines to interpret and understand the visual world. This capability is applied in autonomous vehicles, facial recognition systems, and surveillance systems to identify objects, people, scenes, and activities.

7. Predictive Analytics: AI is used for forecasting future trends and behaviors, allowing businesses and governments to make proactive decisions. This includes predicting consumer behavior, weather forecasting, and anticipating maintenance needs in manufacturing.

8. Robotics: AI drives the operation of robots in manufacturing, space exploration, and health care. These robots can perform tasks that are hazardous or beyond human capabilities, from defusing bombs to performing precise surgical operations.

9. Creative Design and Content Generation: Generative AI models are used for creating art, music, writing, and design, pushing the boundaries of creativity by collaborating with humans or autonomously generating novel creations.

10. Environmental Monitoring and Conservation: AI helps monitor environmental data, predict changes, and develop conservation strategies. It is used to track wildlife populations, analyze forest coverage using satellite images, and model climate change impacts.

11. Educational Applications: AI personalizes learning experiences for students by adapting content to their learning pace and style, providing assistance through tutoring systems, and automating grading.

These examples illustrate just a fraction of the ways in which AI is employed to solve problems, optimize processes, and enhance the capabilities of various industries and sectors globally. As technology advances, the range and complexity of problems that AI can tackle will continue to expand.

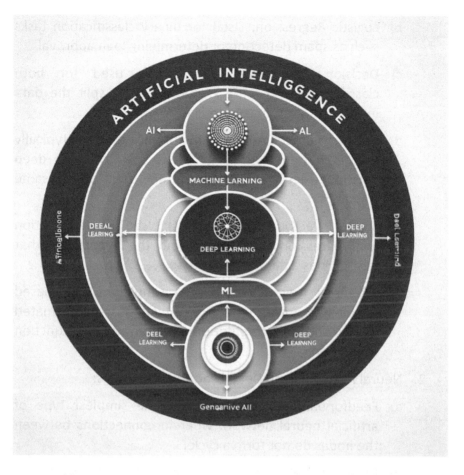

This is what Dall-E generated for the previous image.
It's a very impressive image, but it's wrong. Don't trust computers, the Internet, or AI to be correct.

Artificial intelligence (AI) employs a wide array of algorithms based on the specific tasks and challenges at hand. Here are some of the most common algorithms used across various domains of AI:

1. Machine Learning Algorithms:

   a) Linear Regression: Used for predicting a dependent variable using a linear relationship with one or more independent variables.

b) Logistic Regression: Used for binary classification tasks such as spam detection or determining loan approval.

c) Decision Trees: Versatile models used for both classification and regression tasks. They split the data into branches to make predictions.

d) Random Forests: An ensemble of decision trees typically used to tackle overfitting by averaging multiple deep decision trees trained on different parts of the same training set.

e) Support Vector Machines (SVM): Used for classification and regression tasks, SVMs find the hyperplane that best divides a dataset into classes.

f) K-Nearest Neighbors (KNN): A simple, instance-based learning algorithm where the function is approximated locally and all computation is deferred until function evaluation.

2. Neural Networks and Deep Learning Algorithms:

a) Feedforward Neural Networks: The simplest type of artificial neural network wherein connections between the nodes do not form a cycle.

b) Convolutional Neural Networks (CNNs): Deep learning algorithms that take an input image, assign importance (learnable weights and biases) to various aspects/objects in the image, and differentiate one from the other.

c) Recurrent Neural Networks (RNNs): Used for sequential data like time series or natural language.

d) Long Short-term Memory Networks (LSTMs): A special kind of RNN, capable of learning long-term dependencies.

e) Generative Adversarial Networks (GANs): Consist of two neural networks, the generator and the discriminator, which compete against each other to generate new data with the same statistics as the training set.

3. Optimization Algorithms:

a) Gradient Descent: Used to minimize the cost function in a neural network by updating the parameters in the opposite direction of the gradient.

> **Impact on Society**
>
> **AI has a profound impact on various aspects of society, including economic growth, employment, health care, ethics, privacy, and social interaction. It presents both opportunities and challenges that require careful consideration.**

b) Genetic Algorithms: Based on the process of natural selection, these algorithms reflect the process of natural evolution, simulating the survival of the fittest among individual solutions over consecutive generations for solving optimization problems.

4. Probabilistic Algorithms:

a) Naive Bayes Classifier: A simple probabilistic classifier based on applying Bayes' theorem with strong (naive) independence assumptions between the features.

b) Hidden Markov Models (HMMs): Used in temporal pattern recognition such as speech, handwriting, gesture recognition, part-of-speech tagging, musical score following, partial discharges, and bioinformatics.

5. Reinforcement Learning Algorithms:

a) Q-Learning: An off-policy learner that learns the value of an action in a particular state.

b) Deep Q Networks (DQN): Combining Q-Learning with deep neural networks, DQN uses experience replay and target networks to stabilize the learning algorithm.

Each of these algorithms serves different purposes and is chosen based on the complexity of the task, the nature of the data, and the specific requirements of the application. They are fundamental tools in the AI practitioner's arsenal, enabling machines to make decisions and predictions, recognize patterns, and automate tasks across various industries.

Machine Learning (ML)

ML, a subset of AI, focuses on developing algorithms that allow machines to learn from and make predictions or decisions based on data. Unlike traditional programming, which requires explicit instructions for each task, ML systems improve automatically through experience. ML is further categorized into supervised learning, unsupervised learning, and reinforcement learning, each with distinct mechanisms and applications.

> If we have a choice between a generalized LLM and a narrow AI task-specific service, we will usually choose the narrow AI task-specific service because it has been fine-tuned to preform that specific task.
>
> You can do something similar with a generalized LLM by creating a set of finely tuned prompts on a single subject.

Here are several key types of problems that machine learning is commonly used to solve:

1. Classification: This involves predicting the category to which a data point belongs. Machine learning models can be trained to classify emails as spam or not spam, diagnose diseases based on symptoms, or identify customer sentiment from reviews.

2. Regression: Regression problems involve predicting a continuous value. For instance, machine learning can estimate house prices based on location and features, forecast stock prices, or predict temperature from historical weather data.

3. Clustering: Clustering algorithms are used to group a set of objects in such a way that objects in the same group are more similar to each other than to those in other groups. Examples include customer segmentation in marketing strategies, grouping genes with similar expression patterns in bioinformatics, or organizing articles that cover similar topics.

4. Anomaly Detection: Machine learning can be used to identify rare items, events, or observations that raise suspicions by differing significantly from the majority of the data. This is useful in credit card fraud detection, network intrusion detection, or spotting defective products in manufacturing.

5. Dimensionality Reduction: Reducing the number of random variables to consider by obtaining a set of principal variables. Techniques like PCA (principal component analysis) are used to simplify the data without losing critical information, which can be crucial for improving model accuracy and reducing computational costs.

6. Recommendation Systems: Machine learning powers recommendation engines that suggest products, movies, or songs to users based on their past preferences and behaviors. This is extensively used in e-commerce and entertainment (Netflix, Amazon, Spotify).

7. Natural Language Processing (NLP): From speech recognition, translating between languages, and generating responses in chatbots to more complex tasks like sentiment

analysis or summarizing large documents, machine learning is at the core of modern NLP.

8. Computer Vision: Machine learning algorithms, especially deep learning, are fundamental in enabling computers to see, identify, and process images at a high level and perform tasks such as facial recognition, optical character recognition (OCR), or object detection.

9. Predictive Maintenance: Utilizing historical data to predict when maintenance should be performed on machines and which can prevent unexpected machine failures and extend the life of the manufacturing equipment.

10. Automating Decision-making: ML can automate complex decision-making processes by analyzing large datasets to identify trends and patterns that are not apparent to human analysts. This can be applied in areas such as financial trading, resource allocation in large projects, or strategic planning.

Machine learning's flexibility and adaptability make it a powerful tool for deriving value from vast and varied datasets across practically every industry, from health care to finance, retail, and beyond, transforming data into actionable insights.

Machine learning encompasses a wide range of algorithms, each suited for particular types of data and problems. Here are some of the most commonly used machine learning algorithms:

1. Linear Regression: This algorithm models the relationship between a scalar dependent variable and one or more independent variables using a linear approach. It's widely used for predicting numerical values.

2. Logistic Regression: Despite its name, logistic regression is used for classification problems, not regression. It predicts the probability of occurrence of an event by fitting data to a logistic function.

3. Decision Trees: This model uses a tree-like graph of decisions and their possible consequences. It's simple to understand and interpret and is used for classification and regression tasks.

> **Understanding AI**
>
> **Demystifying AI involves clarifying concepts, terminology, and addressing misconceptions.**

4. Random Forests: An ensemble method that builds multiple decision trees and merges them together to get a more accurate and stable prediction. It's great for both classification and regression.

5. Support Vector Machines (SVM): This algorithm finds a hyperplane in an N-dimensional space (N—the number of features) that distinctly classifies the data points. It's powerful for classification problems, especially binary classification.

6. K-Nearest Neighbors (KNN): KNN algorithm uses 'feature similarity' to predict the values of new datapoints, meaning that the new data point will be assigned a value based on how closely it matches the points in the training set. It can be used for both classification and regression.

7. Naive Bayes: A family of probabilistic algorithms that use Bayes' theorem with the assumption of independence between predictors. Naive Bayes is easy to build and particularly useful for large datasets. It's mostly used in text classification.

8. K-Means Clustering: A type of unsupervised learning that is used when you have unlabeled data. The goal of this algorithm is to find groups in the data, with the number of groups represented by the variable K.

9. Principal Component Analysis (PCA): Used in exploratory data analysis and for making predictive models. It is a statistical procedure that uses an orthogonal transformation

to convert a set of observations of possibly correlated variables into a set of values of linearly uncorrelated variables.

10. Gradient Boosting Machines (GBM): Like Random Forest, GBM is another ensemble technique that builds decision trees sequentially, each new tree correcting errors made by the previously trained tree. It's often considered one of the most powerful techniques for building predictive models, especially for structured data.

Each algorithm has its strengths and weaknesses, and the choice of algorithm typically depends on the specific requirements and constraints of the application, including the nature of the data and the computational resources available.

Deep Learning

Deep learning (DL), a more specific subset of ML, employs neural networks with multiple layers (hence "deep") to learn complex patterns in large data sets. This approach is particularly powerful for tasks such as image and speech recognition or natural language processing and is behind many of AI's most notable recent advancements.

> "AI is probably the most important thing humanity has ever worked on. I think of it as something more profound than electricity or fire."
>
> **Sundar Pichai, CEO of Google**

DL is particularly effective at solving problems that involve large amounts of unstructured data and require the identification of intricate patterns and relationships. Here are some types of problems that deep learning is commonly used to solve:

1. Image and Video Recognition: DL excels in tasks such as object detection, facial recognition, and image classification. It's widely used in security systems, automotive systems

(like autonomous driving), and health care diagnostics, where it can help identify diseases from medical imaging.

2. Natural Language Processing (NLP): Deep learning algorithms are fundamental in translating languages, generating text, and understanding human speech. Applications include chatbots, voice-activated assistants, and sentiment analysis tools that interpret customer feedback.

3. Speech Recognition: Technologies like voice-activated GPS systems, hands-free computing, and virtual assistants (like Siri and Alexa) rely on deep learning to accurately convert spoken words into text.

4. Predictive Analytics: Deep learning can forecast trends and behaviors by analyzing data over time. This is useful in stock trading algorithms, demand forecasting in retail, or predictive maintenance in manufacturing.

5. Anomaly Detection: In cybersecurity or fraud detection, deep learning helps identify unusual patterns or anomalies that could indicate a security breach or fraudulent activity. It's also used in industrial settings to detect irregular machine behavior that might signify a need for repairs.

6. Personalization Technology: Deep learning drives recommendation systems that suggest products, movies, or music based on individual preferences. These are used extensively by online retailers and streaming services.

7. Game Playing and Simulations: Deep learning models have been developed to play and excel at complex games such as Go or chess, which involve strategic thinking and planning.

8. Drug Discovery and Genomics: Deep learning aids in understanding genetic sequences and predicting molecular behavior, which can accelerate drug discovery and personalized medicine.

By automating the extraction of complex patterns and predictions from big data, DL enables solutions that are not only efficient but also highly scalable, making it a cornerstone technology in numerous industries.

Here are some of the most popular and widely used DL algorithms:

1. Convolutional Neural Networks (CNNs): These are especially powerful for processing pixel data and are commonly used in image and video recognition, image classification, medical image analysis, and natural language processing. CNNs excel at capturing spatial hierarchies in data by using convolutional layers, making them efficient in handling data with multiple dimensions such as images.

2. Recurrent Neural Networks (RNNs): Ideal for processing sequential data, RNNs are used in speech recognition, natural language processing, and time series prediction. Unlike feedforward neural networks, RNNs have loops allowing information to persist, simulating a form of memory. This makes them suitable for tasks where context and time are crucial.

3. Long Short-term Memory Networks (LSTMs): A special kind of RNN, LSTMs are designed to avoid the long-term dependency problem, allowing them to remember information for long periods. They are fundamental in complex sequential tasks like language translation, speech recognition, and even generating text based on images.

4. Autoencoders: These are used for learning efficient codings of unlabeled data (unsupervised learning). They work by compressing the input into a latent-space representation and then reconstructing the output from this representation. Autoencoders are widely used for anomaly detection, image reconstruction, and feature extraction.

5. Generative Adversarial Networks (GANs): Consisting of two neural networks—the generator and the discriminator—GANs are used in image generation, video generation, and voice generation. The generator creates data that is indistinguishable from real data, while the discriminator tries to distinguish between real and generated data. This setup enables them to generate high-quality, realistic images or videos.

6. Transformer Models: Although not initially categorized under traditional neural network architectures, transformers have recently become very popular, especially in handling sequential data for tasks like natural language understanding and generation. The transformer model, which uses mechanisms called attention and self-attention, allows for much more parallelization than RNNs and has been pivotal in the success of models like BERT, GPT (from OpenAI), T5, and others in processing language tasks.

These algorithms each have unique strengths, making them suited to different types of data and tasks. Their applications continue to expand as research progresses in the field of deep learning.

> **"Artificial Intelligence has the potential to transform how we live, work, and communicate."**
>
> **Kai-Fu Lee**

Generative AI

Generative AI refers to AI techniques capable of generating new content and data that resembles the training data. This can include creating realistic images, videos, music, or text. Techniques such as Generative adversarial networks (GANs) and variational autoencoders (VAEs) are prominent examples of generative AI models. These models find applications in fields ranging from content creation to data augmentation.

Here are some key applications:

1. Content Generation: Generative AI is extensively used in media and entertainment for generating realistic images, videos, music, and textual content. This can include everything from creating new artwork in specific styles to generating novel music compositions or writing creative fiction.

2. Data Augmentation: In fields where data can be scarce or expensive to acquire, such as medical imaging, generative AI models can produce additional synthetic data. This helps improve the performance of machine learning models by providing a larger dataset for training.

3. Drug Discovery: Generative models can predict molecular structures that could lead to new pharmaceuticals, significantly speeding up the process of drug discovery and development. They simulate how different chemical compounds might interact with biological targets to assess potential efficacy and safety.

4. Personalized Content and Recommendations: Generative AI can tailor content to individual tastes and preferences in digital marketing and entertainment platforms, enhancing user engagement through personalized advertisements, product recommendations, and content curation.

5. Simulation and Scenario Analysis: Generative AI can simulate different scenarios in virtual environments, useful for training AI models, planning urban development, or preparing for emergency response. It allows for testing in a risk-free environment, making it invaluable for strategic planning and training.

6. Language Translation: Generative models are at the forefront of improving machine translation, helping translate languages with greater accuracy and fluency, which is crucial for global communication and business.

7. Fashion and Design: In the creative industries, generative AI can produce new designs for clothing, interior decor, or even architecture, providing professionals with novel ideas and conceptual directions.

8. Game Development: Generative AI can be used to create realistic game environments, character dialogues, and plot variations, enhancing the gaming experience by offering dynamic and engaging content.

9. Anomaly Detection: By learning to generate typical data patterns, generative AI can also identify anomalies or outliers, which is crucial in cybersecurity, fraud detection, and monitoring industrial processes.

> "We are entering a new world where artificial intelligence is powering machines that can understand humans and respond to them, opening up an entirely new era of human-machine interaction."
>
> **Ginni Rometty,**
> **former CEO of IBM**

10. Educational Tools: Generative AI can create educational content that is customized to the learning pace and style of individual students, including generating practice problems, explanations, and interactive learning modules.

Generative AI's ability to create and innovate makes it a powerful tool for addressing a wide range of problems, driving both efficiency and creativity across various sectors.

Generative AI encompasses several algorithms, each with unique capabilities for creating new data and content. Here are some of the most common and impactful algorithms used in generative AI:

1. Generative Adversarial Networks (GANs): Perhaps the most famous generative model, GANs consist of two neural networks—the generator and the discriminator—competing

against each other. The generator creates data aiming to mimic the true data distribution, while the discriminator evaluates whether the data is real or produced by the generator. This process improves both networks until the generator produces realistic outputs. GANs are widely used for image generation, style transfer, and more.

2. Variational Autoencoders (VAEs): VAEs are another popular type of generative model that uses an encoder-decoder architecture. The encoder compresses the input into a latent space, and the decoder reconstructs the output from this compressed representation. VAEs are particularly good at generating new images, enhancing collaborative filtering, and performing anomaly detection.

3. Autoregressive Models: These models predict future values in a sequence by learning the dependencies between the elements. Examples include PixelRNN and PixelCNN, which generate images pixel by pixel. In natural language processing (NLP), models like GPT (Generative Pre-trained Transformer) use autoregressive techniques to generate coherent text based on the previous tokens in a sequence.

4. Transformer-based Models: While originally designed for NLP tasks, transformers have been adapted for generative tasks due to their ability to handle long-range dependencies within data. Models like GPT-4 and other variants are used extensively for generating text, code, and even for tasks like image generation through adaptations like DALL-E.

5. Normalizing Flows: This class of generative models provides a way to transform data from a complex distribution into a simpler distribution (usually Gaussian) using a series of invertible transformations. This makes it possible to model the probability density of data effectively, which is useful in tasks requiring detailed likelihood evaluations, such as scientific simulations and detailed image synthesis.

6. Diffusion Models: These are a newer class of generative models that convert noise into data through a gradual denoising process. They have been shown to produce high-quality images and are considered competitive with GANs in terms of the fidelity and diversity of the generated samples. Models like Google's Imagen and OpenAI's DALL-E use diffusion techniques for state-of-the-art image generation.

Each of these algorithms has unique strengths, making them suitable for different types of generative tasks across various domains, from art and design to scientific research and beyond.

In summary, while AI includes a broad set of techniques for mimicking human intelligence, ML is focused specifically on learning from data. Deep learning dives deeper into complex data learning through advanced neural networks, and Generative AI focuses on creating new, realistic outputs based on learned data patterns. Understanding these distinctions clarifies the capabilities and limitations of each technology within the AI landscape.

Time for a Deep Breath!

It's perfectly natural to feel a bit overwhelmed as you navigate through the myriad of terms and concepts introduced in this chapter. AI, much like any advanced field of study, comes with its own language—terms like "NLP" (natural language processing), "GPT" (Generative Pre-trained Transformer), and others are the building blocks for understanding how AI can revolutionize business practices.

Remember, the goal of this chapter isn't to turn you into a theoretical AI researcher, but to start building your familiarity with AI terminology. It's okay if you don't remember all the terms right away or understand their intricacies on your first read. This is a starting point, and like any new skill, it gets easier with practice and exposure.

I encourage you to treat this chapter as a reference—something you can return to periodically. Each time you come back, you might find that terms which once seemed foreign are now more understandable. Over time, you'll recognize these terms in the context of your business or when they pop up in news articles or discussions about technology. This familiarity will not only make the rest of this book more accessible but will also empower you to think critically about how AI can be integrated into your operations.

Take a deep breath, and when you're ready, try reading through the chapter again. Each pass through the information will help cement your understanding and boost your confidence. Remember, every expert was once a beginner, and your journey into the world of AI starts with these first few steps.

Beyond the Hype: Realistic Expectations and Common Fears

As businesses embark on integrating AI, it's crucial to navigate this landscape with a balanced perspective. While AI offers immense potential, setting realistic expectations and addressing common fears is essential for successful implementation.

Realistic Expectations

Incremental Progress: AI adoption should be viewed as a gradual enhancement rather than an instant transformation. It's about progressively improving existing processes and decision-making capabilities. Start small, iterate, and continuously improve.

Customization and Integration: AI solutions should be tailored to meet specific business needs and integrated seamlessly with existing systems. Off-the-shelf AI tools often require customization to achieve the best results.

Data Quality and Availability: The success of AI depends heavily on the quality and quantity of the data available. Businesses must invest in robust data infrastructure to ensure that their data is clean, relevant, and readily accessible.

Skill Development: Effective AI implementation requires a certain level of technical expertise. Businesses should either focus on upskilling their workforce or collaborate with AI specialists to fully leverage the technology.

Common Misconceptions and Fears about AI

AI is synonymous with robots: While robots can indeed be enhanced by AI, the scope of AI extends far beyond robotics. AI encompasses a broad array of technologies, including software algorithms, data analysis systems, and virtual assistants—none of which require a physical, robotic form.

AI can fully replicate human intelligence: Despite advancements, current AI technologies do not approach the complexity of general AI, which would necessitate machines exhibiting consciousness and emotional understanding. Today's AI systems are primarily designed to excel at specific tasks and do not possess the broad, adaptable cognitive abilities that humans have.

AI will lead to mass unemployment: The introduction of AI, like any major technological innovation, may shift the employment landscape by automating certain tasks. However, it also fosters new job opportunities and industries. The overall impact on employment will largely depend on societal adaptation and the integration of AI technologies into the economy, echoing the transformative effects of historical advancements like the wheel, electricity, and the Internet. For businesses struggling to find sufficient employees, AI can reassign rather than displace staff, helping to address workforce shortages.

AI is always objective and unbiased: AI systems, in reality, can manifest biases present in their training data or the assumptions built into their algorithms. These biases can lead to outcomes that are unfair or discriminatory. Recognizing and mitigating these biases is a critical aspect of responsible AI development.

Loss of Control: There is a fear that AI systems might operate beyond human oversight. Establishing clear governance and ethical guidelines can mitigate this concern, ensuring that AI operates within well-defined boundaries and always incorporates human feedback on its performance.

Security and Privacy: With AI systems processing vast amounts of data, data security and privacy become paramount. Implementing stringent security measures and complying with privacy regulations are essential to maintaining trust in AI technologies.

In conclusion, by approaching AI with realistic expectations and proactively addressing common fears, businesses can effectively navigate the complexities of AI integration. By emphasizing incremental progress through customization, data integrity, and skill development and tackling concerns regarding job displacement, control, bias, and security, organizations can unlock AI's transformative potential while safeguarding against its risks.

How AI Differs from Traditional Programming

Understanding the distinction between artificial intelligence (AI) and traditional programming is crucial for businesses aiming to leverage AI effectively. While both involve coding and software development, their approaches and underlying principles differ significantly.

Traditional Programming

Rule-Based Logic: Traditional programming relies on developers writing explicit instructions or rules that the computer strictly follows to perform tasks. The outcomes are entirely dependent on the predefined logic and the given inputs.

Limited Adaptability: Once written, traditional programs perform the same tasks in the same manner unless manually updated. They lack the capability to adapt or learn from new data autonomously.

Predictable Outcomes: The results from traditional programs are predictable and deterministic, provided that the inputs and the logic do not change.

Artificial Intelligence (AI)

Learning from Data: AI systems, especially those based on machine learning, learn to identify patterns and relationships within data. Instead of relying on explicitly programmed instructions, they develop their own logic or rules to make predictions or decisions.

Adaptability and Evolution: AI systems are designed to continuously improve and adapt by learning from new data. This ongoing learning process allows them to refine their algorithms over time, enhancing their accuracy and effectiveness.

Handling Uncertainty and Complexity: AI excels in tasks involving uncertainty, complexity, or non-linear relationships, which are challenging for traditional programming methods. This capability is particularly useful in areas like natural language processing and image recognition.

Decision-making and Predictive Capabilities: Unlike traditional programs, AI systems can make decisions or predictions based on probabilistic reasoning, even when faced with incomplete or ambiguous data. This marks a significant shift from the deterministic nature of traditional programming.

In summary, while traditional programming is centered around strict rules and deterministic outcomes, AI uses data-driven learning to identify patterns and make decisions. This fundamental difference equips AI to address complex challenges, adapt to evolving situations, and provide insights beyond the reach of conventional programming. For businesses, grasping this distinction is essential for effectively deploying AI to drive innovation and tackle real-world problems.

Part 2:
AI in Business

"The real value of AI in business is not in the technology itself, but in the ways it can help us make better decisions, faster and with greater accuracy."

— Andrew Ng, Co-founder of Google Brain

Chapter 3:
Why Businesses Need AI

Introduction

In today's fast-paced business world, companies are constantly facing new challenges and opportunities. As technology advances, so do customer expectations and the complexity of operations.

This is where artificial intelligence (AI) comes into play. AI is not just a buzzword or a distant future concept; it's a practical tool that is already transforming the way businesses operate and compete.

This chapter delves into the various problems that AI can solve for businesses, from predicting customer behavior to optimizing supply chains. AI is proving to be an invaluable asset in addressing some of the most pressing issues faced by companies today. We will explore how AI can enhance customer service, streamline operations, detect fraud, and much more. By understanding the potential of AI, businesses can leverage this technology to solve problems, improve efficiency, and ultimately achieve greater success.

Problems AI Can Solve for Businesses

AI is like a super-smart assistant capable of analyzing vast amounts of data quickly, making it ideal for tackling complex business challenges:

Solving Complex Problems: AI excels in areas like predicting customer behavior, optimizing supply chains, and detecting fraud. By addressing these issues, businesses can enhance decision-making, reduce costs, and boost efficiency.

Enhancing Customer Experience: AI helps businesses better understand their customers and provide personalized experiences. For instance, AI-powered chatbots can handle inquiries 24/7, and recommendation systems can tailor product suggestions to individual preferences, enhancing customer

> AI improves business operations by automating routine tasks, optimizing supply chains, and analyzing vast amounts of data for better decision-making. This leads to cost reduction, increased productivity, and improved efficiency.

satisfaction and allowing human agents to focus on more complex tasks. It can also forecast future behaviors, aiding in personalized marketing, inventory management, and proactive customer service.

Boosting Innovation: AI fosters innovation by helping to develop new products while improving existing ones and creating new business models—keeping companies at the forefront of their industries.

Improving Decision-making: AI enhances decision-making by analyzing data to identify patterns and insights, helping businesses capitalize on opportunities and minimize risks.

Streamlining Operations: AI automates routine tasks like data entry and inventory management, increasing productivity and reducing errors.

Detecting Fraud: By analyzing transaction patterns, AI helps flag suspicious activities, preventing fraud and protecting both businesses and their customers.

Optimizing Supply Chains: AI enhances supply chain management by forecasting demand, optimizing delivery routes, and managing inventory levels, ensuring efficient and cost-effective operations.

Enhancing Marketing Efforts: AI improves marketing strategies by analyzing data to identify target audiences, predict trends, and optimize campaigns, ensuring that marketing efforts are more effective.

Boosting Sales: AI helps increase sales by identifying potential leads, personalizing sales approaches, and predicting popular products, ultimately enhancing the bottom line.

Optimizing Pricing Strategies: AI analyzes market trends, competitor prices, and customer demand to help set optimal pricing strategies, maximizing profits while staying competitive.

Managing Human Resources: AI aids in recruiting by analyzing resumes, identifying top candidates, and predicting employee turnover, streamlining HR processes and ensuring a talented workforce.

Improving Product Development: AI reduces the risks associated with new products by analyzing market trends, customer feedback, and competitor actions, informing more successful product innovations.

By leveraging AI across these diverse areas, businesses can achieve significant advantages, transforming operations and driving growth in a competitive landscape.

Overview of AI Algorithms and Tools

Artificial intelligence (AI) utilizes a diverse array of algorithms and tools, each tailored to address specific problems or tasks. Below is an overview of some key AI algorithms and the tools commonly used in AI applications:

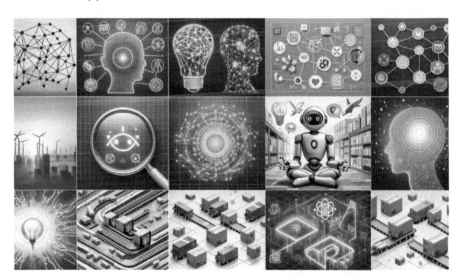

AI Algorithms
Supervised Learning Algorithms:

Linear Regression: Predicts a continuous value, such as sales forecasting.

Logistic Regression: Handles binary classification tasks, like spam detection.

Decision Trees: Useful for classification and regression tasks, such as customer segmentation.

Random Forests: An ensemble method that improves accuracy using multiple decision trees, applied in credit risk assessment.

Support Vector Machines (SVM): Employed for classification and regression tasks, including image classification.

Unsupervised Learning Algorithms:

K-Means Clustering: Groups data into clusters, used for market segmentation.

Hierarchical Clustering: Creates a tree of clusters, which is useful for taxonomy creation.

Apriori Algorithm: Generates association rules commonly used in market basket analysis.

Reinforcement Learning Algorithms:

Q-Learning: Aims at decision-making in uncertain environments, such as in gaming.

Deep Q Network (DQN): Integrates Q-learning with deep neural networks, which is used in autonomous driving.

Policy Gradient Methods: Optimizes policies directly, applicable in robotic control.

Deep Learning Algorithms:

Convolutional Neural Networks (CNNs): Ideal for image and video recognition tasks like facial recognition.

Recurrent Neural Networks (RNNs): Analyzes sequential data and is used in language translation.

Long Short-term Memory (LSTM): A type of RNN designed for processing longer sequences, applicable in text generation.

Generative Adversarial Networks (GANs): Generates new data samples, such as synthetic images.

Natural Language Processing (NLP) Algorithms:

Tokenization, stemming, and lemmatization: Essential for text preprocessing.

Bag of Words, TF-IDF: Techniques for representing text data.

AI personalizes customer interactions through chatbots and recommendation systems, enhancing customer satisfaction. Additionally, AI fosters innovation by aiding in the development of new products and business models, keeping companies competitive.

Word2Vec, BERT: Advanced methods for creating word embeddings and contextual representations.

AI Tools and Platforms
Microsoft

Microsoft Azure AI: Offers a comprehensive suite of AI services, including machine learning and cognitive services.

Cognitive Services: Provides pre-built AI capabilities such as vision, speech, and language processing to applications.

Azure Machine Learning: A cloud-based platform for building, training, and deploying machine learning models.

Open Neural Network Exchange (ONNX): Facilitates model interoperability across different AI frameworks.

ML.NET: A cross-platform, open-source machine learning framework for .NET developers.

AutoML: Tools like Azure AutoML and Google AutoML that automate the selection of the best models and parameters.

Semantic Kernel: Enhances natural language processing tasks by understanding and interpreting human language.

CoPilot: Assists developers by suggesting code snippets and automating repetitive programming tasks.

Power Platform: Includes tools such as Power BI, Power Apps, and Power Automate, enriching them with AI capabilities.

AWS AI Services

Amazon's suite includes Amazon SageMaker for building and training models, Amazon Rekognition for image analysis, Textract for OCR, Transcribe, Translate, Comprehend for NLP, Comprehend Medical for medical NLP, and Anthropic Claude for LLM.

AWS is probably the second AI platform we use. It has an excellent Visual Studio add-in and .NET SDKs for calling all AWS services. These make it very easy to use AWS.

Google Cloud AI

Provides machine learning services and APIs for tasks like image analysis and natural language processing.

We use Google when we need data related to "Search," but Google also has very good AI services and APIs.

Libraries

TorchSharp and SciSharp: .NET libraries providing interfaces to machine learning frameworks like PyTorch and TensorFlow.

TensorFlow and PyTorch: Open-source libraries for machine learning, widely used for research and production in academia and industry.

Scikit-learn and Keras: Popular Python libraries for machine learning, providing easy-to-use interfaces for data mining and neural networks.

This comprehensive array of AI algorithms and tools enables businesses to harness the transformative power of AI across various applications and industries.

Diverse AI Algorithms for Various Applications

AI algorithms encompass a range of techniques for different tasks, including supervised learning (e.g., linear regression for sales forecasting, decision trees for customer segmentation), unsupervised learning (e.g., K-means clustering for market segmentation), reinforcement learning (e.g., Q-learning for decision-making in gaming), deep learning (e.g., CNNs for image recognition, LSTMs for text generation), and natural language processing (e.g., BERT for creating contextual word embeddings).

Chapter 4:
AI in Action

"Creativity is just connecting things. When you ask creative people how they did something, they feel a little guilty because they didn't really do it, they just saw something. It seemed obvious to them after a while. That's because they were able to connect experiences they've had and synthesize new things."

— Steve Jobs

Introduction

In the previous chapter, we explored the problems that AI can solve for businesses. But how does this translate into real-world applications? Chapter 4 takes you on a journey through various industries, showcasing how AI is not just a theoretical concept but a practical tool that is already reshaping the business landscape. In this chapter, we'll delve into specific use cases and applications of AI, illustrating how businesses are leveraging this technology to gain a competitive edge and drive innovation.

The Goal of this Chapter

In the dynamic landscape of business technology, AI stands as a beacon of innovation, offering myriad applications that can revolutionize how businesses operate. Recognizing the diversity and potential specificity of business needs, this book meticulously catalogs hundreds of AI applications. This extensive list is not a showcase of possibilities but a strategic tool designed to bridge the gap between theoretical AI capabilities and practical, actionable solutions for businesses.

The phenomenon of connecting ideas from the book to a business's specific challenges and opportunities is grounded in the concept of "relevant resonance." As readers peruse through various AI applications, from predictive analytics to customer service bots, they are encouraged to identify and align these solutions with their unique business contexts. You can adapt these AI applications to improve your business's operational efficiency, innovation, and competitive edge.

> **Start Small and Scale**
>
> **Pilot Projects: Begin with small, manageable projects to test the new technology's feasibility.**
>
> **Iterative Approach: Use an agile methodology to iteratively develop and refine solutions.**

Moreover, this approach democratizes AI technology, making it accessible and applicable to businesses of all sizes and sectors. By providing a broad spectrum of applications, the book empowers business leaders, strategists, and IT professionals to envision and implement AI-driven transformations tailored to their specific needs.

This not only facilitates a deeper understanding of AI's potential but also sparks innovation through the cross-pollination of ideas between different industries and domains. In essence, the book serves as a catalyst for innovation, prompting businesses to think creatively about how AI can be harnessed to not just incrementally improve but fundamentally change the way they operate.

Please don't just skim through these AI examples. For each one, pause and consider: With a few adjustments, could this AI application be beneficial to my business?

Your objective for this chapter is to carefully analyze each AI application and to consider how it could be adapted to suit your business. Reflect on the necessary modifications and potential benefits each could bring. Document your insights and plans in a structured format, such as a spreadsheet or a detailed document.

AI Use Cases and Applications You May Already Be Using

People increasingly utilize AI in their daily lives, often without realizing the extent of its integration. Here's a list of how AI seamlessly enhances everyday activities, showcasing its widespread adoption:

1. Smartphone Features:
   a) Face ID and biometric unlocking
   b) Digital voice assistants for tasks like setting reminders and making calls

2. Social Media:
   a) Personalized feeds
   b) Fake news detection
   c) Cyberbullying prevention

3. Communication:
   a) AI-powered grammar and spell-check tools

b) Spam filters in email services

4. Internet Search:

   a) AI-driven search engines

   b) Personalized advertising based on user preferences

5. Entertainment and Media:

   a) Music and video recommendations on platforms like Spotify and Netflix

6. Productivity Tools:

   a) Smart Reply in Gmail for quick email responses

   b) Reminder nudges in Gmail

7. Navigation and Travel:

   a) Parking difficulty predictions in Google Maps

   b) Travel itinerary planning in apps like Google Trips

Build a Skilled Team

Upskill Employees: Provide training programs to enhance your team's skills in new technologies.

Hire Experts: Consider hiring consultants or experts for specific technologies to speed up adoption and implementation.

---

8. Health and Safety:

   a) Fall detection in devices like the Apple Watch

   b) Car crash detection for emergency notifications

9. Gaming and Recreation:

   a) AI in game development and enhanced gaming experiences

10. Home Automation:

    a) Voice-controlled smart home devices

    b) AI-optimized energy usage and security systems

11. Workout Assistance:

    a) AI suggestions for exercise routines

12. Gardening and Landscaping:

    a) AI suggestions for garden layouts and plant selection

13. Code Debugging:

    a) AI-driven suggestions for fixing coding bugs

14. Online Shopping:

    a) Personalized product recommendations on platforms like Amazon

    b) AI chatbots for customer service

15. Financial Services:

    a) Fraud detection in banking

    b) Personalized investment advice

16. Language Translation:

    a) Instant translation services like Google Translate

17. Virtual Health care:

    a) Telemedicine and health metric monitoring

18. Smart Appliances:

    a) AI-enabled refrigerators that suggest recipes based on contents

    b) Smart thermostats that adjust based on user behavior

19. Personalized Learning:

> **Integrate with Current Systems**
>
> **Compatibility Check: Ensure the new technology integrates well with your existing systems to avoid disruptions.**
>
> **APIs and Connectors: Use them to seamlessly integrate new technology with your current software infrastructure.**

a) Adaptive learning platforms

b) AI tutors for skill enhancement

20. Traffic Management:

a) AI-driven traffic signal control and route suggestions

21. Content Creation:

a) AI tools for generating art, music, or writing

22. Job Search:

a) AI-driven job matching and resume optimization

23. Personal Finance Management.

a) Budgeting and expense tracking with AI apps

24. Home Security:

a) Facial recognition in smart doorbells

b) Unusual activity detection in security cameras

25. Mental Health Support:

a) Chatbots for emotional support

b) Voice analysis for mood pattern detection

26. Personalized Fitness:

a) Custom workout plans from AI fitness apps

27. Weather Forecasting:

a) Accurate AI-driven weather predictions

28. Food and Cooking:

a) Recipe suggestions and meal planning with AI cooking apps

29. Fashion and Style:

a) Personalized style recommendations

b) Virtual try-on features in clothing apps

30. Personalized News:

  a) AI-curated news feeds

  b) Filtering of biased or fake news

31. Time Management:

  a) AI-powered scheduling and productivity analysis

32. Home Renovation:

  a) AI tools for visualizing renovation projects

33. Music Composition:

  a) AI software for creating and remixing music

34. Wearable Health Devices:

  a) Health monitoring and personalized recommendations

> **Focus on Business Value**
>
> **ROI Analysis: Regularly assess the return on investment (ROI) to ensure the technology adds value to your business.**
>
> **Solve Real Problems: Apply technology to address specific business challenges rather than for its own sake.**

35. Environmental Conservation:

  a) Satellite imagery analysis for environmental monitoring

36. Personal Security:

  a) Facial recognition for secure access

  b) Detection of unusual behavior or potential threats

37. Language Learning:

  a) Personalized language learning apps

  b) Pronunciation feedback from AI chatbots

38. Personalized Shopping Recommendations:

a) AI-driven product suggestions based on shopping behavior

39. Smart Energy Management:

    a) AI optimization of home energy use

40. Emotional Intelligence:

    a) Emotional recognition for more empathetic virtual interactions

41. Legal Assistance:

    a) AI tools for legal research and contract review

42. Personalized Travel Recommendations:

    a) AI travel platforms for customized trip planning

43. Home Decor and Design:

    a) Virtual interior design tools

44. AI-Powered Tutoring:

    a) Personalized AI tutoring sessions

45. Automated Personal Finance Management:

    a) AI financial advisors for portfolio management

46. AI-Enhanced Photography:

    a) AI scene recognition in camera apps

47. Personalized Health Care Plans:

    a) Customized health plans from AI health apps

48. AI-Powered Language Translation Devices:

Encourage a Culture of Innovation

Innovation Time: Create time where employees can experiment with new technologies without the fear of failure.

Recognition Programs: Reward employees who contribute innovative ideas and solutions.

a) Real-time translation devices for multilingual communication

49. Virtual Home Assistants:

a) Smart devices like Amazon Echo for home automation

50. AI-Powered Personalized Fitness Coaching:

a) Virtual fitness coaching and performance analysis

51. AI-Driven Personalized Marketing:

a) Targeted advertising campaigns based on AI analysis

These examples highlight the diverse applications of AI across various aspects of life, from everyday convenience to critical decision-making, illustrating AI's transformative impact and potential for future innovations. Businesses can draw insights from these consumer applications to envision new AI solutions tailored to their specific operational needs.

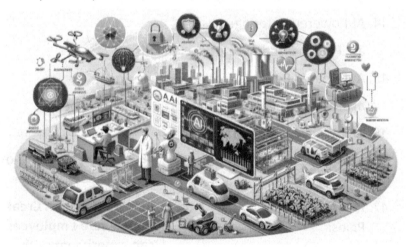

Use Cases and Applications of AI in Various Industries

1. Health Care

a) Disease Diagnosis and Prognosis: Utilizing medical imaging analysis for more accurate diagnoses.

b) Personalized Treatment Plans: Tailoring treatments based on individual patient data.

c) Drug Discovery and Development: Enhancing pharmaceutical research with molecular simulations.

d) Remote Patient Monitoring: Using wearable devices to track patient health in real-time.

e) Predictive Analytics: Leveraging data to predict disease outbreaks and improve public health responses.

f) AI-Assisted Surgery: The da Vinci Surgical System, a robotic platform, enhances surgical precision and control, utilizing AI algorithms to analyze real-time data, thereby aiding surgeons in decision-making during procedures.

g) AI in Disease Detection and Diagnosis: IBM's Watson Health leverages natural language processing and machine learning to analyze medical literature and patient data, helping doctors diagnose complex cases and tailor treatment options.

2. Finance

a) Fraud Detection and Prevention: Identifying and preventing fraudulent activities in banking transactions.

b) Algorithmic Trading: Utilizing market sentiment analysis for automated trading strategies.

c) Credit Scoring and Risk Assessment: Enhancing loan approval processes with AI-driven risk evaluations.

d) Personalized Financial Advice: Providing customized financial planning with robo-advisors.

e) Automated Compliance Monitoring: Streamlining regulatory reporting and compliance checks.

f) AI in Fraud Detection: Mastercard employs AI systems to analyze transaction data in real-time, identifying patterns indicative of fraud and preemptively blocking suspicious transactions.

g) AI for Investment Strategies: Robo-advisors like Wealthfront and Betterment use AI to analyze market trends and manage portfolios, providing personalized investment advice based on individual financial goals and risk tolerance.

3. Retail

a) Personalized Product Recommendations: Customizing shopping experiences for online customers.

b) Inventory Management: Utilizing demand forecasting to optimize stock levels.

c) Customer Sentiment Analysis: Gaining insights into brand perception and customer preferences.

d) Virtual Assistants: Employing chatbots for efficient customer service.

e) Augmented Reality: Enhancing the shopping experience with virtual try-on tools.

f) AI-Powered Personalization: Amazon's recommendation engine utilizes machine learning to analyze browsing and purchase histories, suggesting products that

---

Adopt a User-Centric Approach

User Feedback: Involve end-users early in the process to gather feedback and make necessary adjustments.

Ease of Use: Prioritize user-friendly solutions to ensure higher adoption rates among employees.

---

enhance customer experience and boost sales.

g) AI-Enhanced Supply Chain Management: Walmart uses AI to predict demand, optimize inventory, and streamline logistics, ensuring efficient product stocking and improved customer satisfaction.

4. Manufacturing

a) Predictive Maintenance: Anticipating equipment failures to reduce downtime.

b) Quality Control: Implementing visual inspection systems to ensure product quality.

c) Supply Chain Optimization: Streamlining logistics to enhance efficiency.

d) Autonomous Robots: Automating assembly and material handling.

e) Energy Efficiency: Monitoring and managing energy use to reduce costs.

f) Predictive Maintenance with AI: Siemens utilizes AI-based solutions to analyze sensor data from machinery, predicting potential issues before they cause downtime.

g) AI for Quality Control: BMW employs machine learning to inspect images of car parts during production, identifying defects to ensure high-quality standards.

5. Transportation and Logistics

a) Route Optimization: Enhancing delivery efficiency with advanced mapping algorithms.

b) Autonomous Vehicles: Developing self-driving tech for cargo and passenger transport.

c) Demand Forecasting: Planning public transportation needs based on predictive data.

d) Real-time Tracking: Monitoring shipment locations for improved logistics management.

e) Smart Traffic Management: Reducing congestion and improving urban mobility.

f) Autonomous Vehicles: Companies like Tesla and Waymo develop self-driving cars that use AI to navigate roads safely by recognizing traffic signals and making real-time decisions.

g) AI in Traffic Management: Pittsburgh uses AI-powered traffic signal systems to adjust timings based on real-time traffic conditions, reducing congestion and enhancing vehicle flow.

6. Agriculture

a) Crop Monitoring: Using satellite imagery and drones for precise agriculture assessments.

b) Precision Farming: Applying IoT technology for targeted farming interventions.

c) Automated Irrigation and Pest Control: Optimizing resource usage on farms.

d) Supply Chain Efficiency: Ensuring farm-to-table processes are streamlined and sustainable.

e) Livestock Health Management: Monitoring animal health to prevent diseases and optimize production.

f) AI-Driven Crop Monitoring: John Deere's systems analyze drone-captured images to identify crop stress, enabling targeted interventions to improve yield.

g) AI for Soil and Crop Analysis: AeroFarms uses AI to analyze sensor data, optimizing conditions in vertical farms for sustainable agriculture.

7. Energy

a) Grid Management: Forecasting energy demand for more efficient grid operations.

b) Renewable Energy Optimization: Enhancing the storage and distribution of renewable energy.

> **Ensure Security and Compliance**
>
> **Security Protocols: Implement robust security measures to protect sensitive data.**
>
> **Compliance: Stay informed about relevant regulations and ensure your technology implementations comply with them.**

c) Predictive Maintenance: Preventing outages by anticipating infrastructure failures.

d) Smart Meters: Providing real-time data on consumer energy usage.

e) Carbon Footprint Analysis: Aiding companies in their sustainability efforts.

f) AI in Renewable Energy Management: Google's DeepMind develops AI algorithms to optimize data center cooling systems, enhancing the efficiency of renewable energy use.

g) AI in Grid Management: AutoGrid analyzes data from smart meters using AI, predicting energy demand and optimizing electricity distribution for improved grid efficiency.

8. Education

a) Personalized Learning: Customizing educational content to fit student learning styles.

b) Automated Grading: Streamlining assessment processes with AI.

c) Virtual Reality Simulations: Creating immersive educational experiences.

d) Language Translation Tools: Facilitating global access to educational content.

e) Predictive Analytics: Improving student retention and performance through data analysis.

f) AI Tutoring Systems: Carnegie Learning's MATHia software adapts to individual learning styles and paces, providing personalized instruction in math.

g) AI for Language Learning: Duolingo uses AI to tailor language lessons to users' proficiency and learning speed, making language acquisition more effective.

9. Entertainment and Media

a) Content Recommendations: Tailoring media content to individual preferences on streaming platforms.

b) Scriptwriting and Content Creation: Automating creative processes with NLP.

c) Interactive Gaming: Enhancing user experiences with virtual assistants.

d) Audience Engagement: Analyzing viewer sentiments for targeted marketing.

e) Deepfake Technology: Innovating in special effects and virtual characters for film and TV.

f) AI in Content Creation: Netflix uses AI to analyze viewer preferences and create personalized content recommendations, keeping audiences engaged and satisfied.

10. Real Estate

   a) Market Analysis: Using AI for detailed property valuation and market trend insights.

   b) Virtual Tours: Offering augmented reality experiences to potential buyers.

   c) Investment Predictive Analytics: Identifying lucrative real estate opportunities.

   d) Smart Building Management: Optimizing building operations for energy efficiency.

   e) Automated Leasing: Streamlining the leasing process from tenant screening to contract management.

   f) AI for Property Valuation: Zillow's Zestimate tool employs machine learning to analyze extensive home data, offering instant property valuations to aid buyers and sellers in making informed decisions.

> **Monitor and Adapt**
>
> **Performance Metrics: Continuously monitor key performance indicators (KPIs) to track the technology's impact.**
>
> **Adaptability: Be ready to pivot and adapt your strategy based on performance data and feedback.**

These examples illustrate how AI is being integrated into various sectors, significantly enhancing efficiency, precision, personalization, and decision-making, and driving innovation in traditional and emerging markets.

Top Use Cases for LLMs, ChatGPT, Virtual Assistants

We recommend employing large language models (LLMs) like ChatGPT, Anthropic Claude, and Google Gemini (BARD) as virtual assistants to generate initial drafts. These drafts should then be reviewed, refined, and edited by humans. After extensive experience—potentially involving thousands or tens of thousands of human-reviewed outputs—you may consider using LLM-generated content directly in low-risk applications. This approach ensures that the outputs are reliable and appropriately tailored to your needs.

1. Customer Support:
   a) Handling common customer inquiries
   b) Providing product or service information
   c) Resolving complaints and issues
   d) Guiding customers through troubleshooting steps

2. Sales and Marketing:
   e) Generating leads through engaging questions
   f) Crafting personalized sales pitches
   g) Creating engaging content for social media
   h) Writing promotional emails or newsletters

3. Human Resources:
   a) Assisting in creating job descriptions
   b) Scheduling interviews and meetings
   c) Automating responses to common HR questions
   d) Generating ideas for team-building activities

4. Project Management:
   a) Generating status update templates
   b) Creating task lists from meeting notes

c) Assisting with risk management and mitigation strategies

d) Simplifying project reporting processes

5. Data Analysis and Reporting:

   a) Generating SQL queries

   b) Summarizing research findings

   c) Creating data visualization prompts

   d) Analyzing customer feedback

6. Content Creation:

   a) Blog post topic generation

   b) Drafting outlines for articles or reports

   c) Creating engaging multimedia content ideas

   d) Summarizing lengthy documents or reports

7. Training and Development:

   a) Generating training material content

   b) Creating quizzes and learning assessments

   c) Providing explanations for complex concepts

   d) Suggesting personalized learning resources

8. Legal and Compliance:

   a) Generating standard legal documents

   b) Assisting with compliance checks

   c) Summarizing legal cases or regulations

   d) Drafting responses to legal inquiries

9. Finance and Accounting:

   a) Generating invoice descriptions

   b) Assisting with budget planning

c) Summarizing financial reports

d) Explaining financial terms and concepts

10. IT and Technical Support:

a) Generating scripts for system diagnostics

b) Creating user guides and FAQs for software tools

c) Offering solutions for common technical issues

d) Drafting change logs and technical documentation

11. Strategy and Innovation:

a) Brainstorming session facilitation prompts

b) SWOT analysis generation

c) Trend analysis and industry updates

d) Innovation challenge ideas and prompts

Finding the perfect use case for AI can be challenging at first. However, integrating AI into even the smallest aspects of your business can provide substantial strategic benefits. It signals to investors, customers, and competitors that your company is innovative and forward-thinking. This can enhance your market position, attract top talent, and even lead to operational efficiencies that you might not have anticipated. Think of it as a stepping stone toward larger, more impactful AI applications in the future.

AWS Connect

AWS Connect, a cloud-based contact (call) center solution, integrates several powerful AI tools to enhance customer service and operational efficiency. One of the standout features is Amazon Q, a generative AI-powered assistant designed to assist contact center agents by providing real-time suggestions, contextual information, and recommended actions. This integration helps agents resolve customer issues more quickly and accurately, improving customer satisfaction and reducing call handling times.

Contact Lens for Amazon Connect is another key AI tool that offers advanced conversational analytics. It provides insights into customer interactions by analyzing call and chat transcripts, detecting sentiment, identifying key issues, and monitoring agent performance. This tool helps supervisors proactively address issues and optimize agent training and performance.

Amazon Connect also features AI-powered chatbots and Amazon Lex for building conversational interfaces. These tools enable natural, intuitive self-service experiences for customers, supporting multiple languages and reducing the need for human intervention. This not only enhances customer experience but also lowers operational costs.

Additionally, Amazon Transcribe, Translate and Amazon Polly are integrated to convert speech to text and text to lifelike speech. These services allow for real-time transcription and speech synthesis, which can be used to automate and streamline customer interactions and data entry tasks.

These AI tools collectively transform AWS Connect into a robust, AI-enhanced platform that helps businesses deliver superior customer service while optimizing contact center operations and reducing costs.

Conclusion

In this chapter, we've examined a wide array of AI applications across various industries, showcasing the versatility and transformative potential of AI technology. Each example demonstrated how AI can tackle real-world business challenges, boost operational efficiency, and drive innovation.

Reflect on how these AI solutions might be tailored to meet your specific business needs. Identify opportunities where AI could address particular challenges or unlock new possibilities. This discussion is intended to prompt you to consider potential AI prototypes that could capitalize on AI's capabilities within your organization.

By now, you should have a better understanding of how to integrate AI into your business processes and a roadmap to explore AI prototypes that align with your strategic objectives. We encourage you to revisit this chapter periodically, each time with a deeper focus, to discover additional AI applications and insights. This ongoing process will ensure you continually find innovative ways to deploy AI, enhancing your company's growth and efficiency.

There are strategic benefits of adopting AI, even if the initial applications seem modest. Here's a structured approach:

1. Strategic Positioning

Future-Proofing: Integrating AI, even in small ways, positions the company as forward-thinking and prepared for future technological advancements.

Competitive Edge: By using AI, even in minor processes, can differentiate the company from competitors who are not yet adopting AI.

2. Market Perception

Investor Confidence: Investors are more likely to invest in companies that show they are embracing modern technologies, as it indicates innovation and potential for growth.

Customer Trust: Customers may perceive the company as more reliable and advanced, enhancing brand reputation and trust.

3. Internal Innovation Culture

Learning and Experimentation: Using AI in small projects allows the company to build internal expertise and an innovative culture, which can later scale to larger, more impactful projects.

Talent Attraction: Being an AI-adopting company can attract top tech talent who are eager to work with cutting-edge technologies.

4. Incremental Benefits

Operational Efficiency: Even small AI implementations can streamline processes, reduce costs, or improve accuracy, providing tangible benefits.

Data Utilization: Leveraging AI can help make better use of existing data, uncovering insights that can drive business decisions.

5. Visibility and Awareness

PR and Marketing: Publicizing AI initiatives, no matter how small, can generate positive media coverage and enhance the company's visibility in the market.

Benchmarking: Demonstrating AI use can put pressure on competitors to follow suit, positioning your company as a market leader.

Part 3:
Building AI Applications

"The best way to predict the future is to invent it."

- Alan Kay

Chapter 5:
Developing an AI Prototype

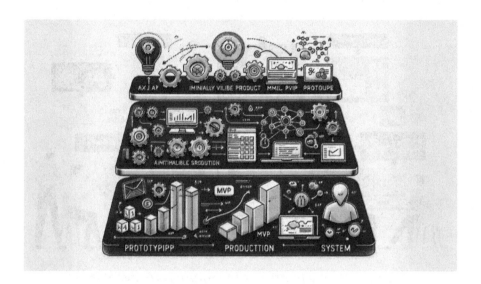

Introduction

Embarking on the journey of developing an AI prototype is both an exciting and challenging endeavor. A prototype is the first tangible manifestation of your AI idea, providing a glimpse into its potential impact and feasibility. This chapter serves as a roadmap for businesses and innovators looking to bring their AI concepts to life.

We will explore the essential steps involved in creating an AI prototype, from ideation and data collection to model selection and integration. This chapter aims to demystify the process, offering practical advice and best practices to guide you through each stage. Whether you're a seasoned developer or new to the world of AI, this chapter will equip you with the knowledge and tools needed to turn your vision into a working prototype.

Developing an AI prototype is not just about technical execution; it's about validating your idea, learning from feedback, and iterating toward a solution that meets real-world needs. By the end of this chapter, you'll be ready to take the first steps in transforming your AI aspirations into reality.

Definitions

Prototype
A prototype is a preliminary model of a product or solution, developed primarily to test and refine ideas during the early stages of creation. It is not a complete version and is generally not ready for public release. Instead, a prototype serves as a tangible proof of concept, used to evaluate the viability of design choices, technical aspects, and overall concept feasibility.

In the realm of AI, a prototype might involve a basic model that illustrates how an AI algorithm can address a specific challenge, though it may not yet be fully integrated or optimized. At this stage, the focus is on exploring the potential and functionality of the idea rather than adhering to best coding practices or formal project management protocols.

This allows stakeholders and subject matter experts (SMEs) to provide valuable feedback without the constraints of rigorous testing, security measures, or task tracking, facilitating rapid iteration and development.

Minimally Viable Product (MVP)
An MVP is a more advanced iteration than a prototype, containing just enough features to engage early adopters and validate the product concept with actual users or in the real market. The primary goal of an MVP is to launch a product swiftly with minimal investment and then collect and analyze user feedback to refine

and enhance the product. Unlike a prototype, an MVP is a functional product that is released to a select group of users.

It is specifically designed to test business hypotheses, understand customer needs, and pinpoint the most crucial features for further development.

In the context of AI, an MVP might consist of a basic application that employs an AI model to address a specific problem, equipped with a straightforward user interface and limited functionality.

> **Define Clear Objectives**
>
> **Specific Goals: Clearly define the problem you are solving and the goals of your AI prototype.**
>
> **Use Cases: Identify specific use cases and scenarios where the AI application will be applied.**

Typically, an MVP covers about 30 percent of the functionality expected in a fully developed product. It may include features such as logging, exception handling, and asynchronous calls to enhance performance and user experience. At this stage, integration into project management and task tracking systems is common, and testing procedures are initiated. Additionally, security reviews are conducted to ensure data integrity and user safety, preparing the MVP for broader user engagement and feedback collection.

Production-Ready Application

A production-ready application is a fully developed product that has been extensively tested and is ready for widespread deployment. It encompasses all essential features, integrations, and optimizations to ensure optimal performance, security, and scalability. This application has passed rigorous testing phases, including user acceptance testing, to guarantee its stability and reliability for live operations.

In the context of AI, a production-ready application represents a complete solution that effectively utilizes an AI model. It features a refined user interface, comprehensive error handling, and seamless integration with other systems or services. The development process for an AI application mirrors that of traditional software, incorporating thorough project management, stringent testing protocols, continuous integration and deployment practices (DevOps), and robust security measures. This holistic approach ensures that the AI application is not only functional but also reliable and secure for end-users.

High-Level Overview

Here is a high-level overview of transitioning from prototype to MVP to a production-ready application, tailored to ensure efficiency and cost-effectiveness at each stage:

1. Identify Promising Use Cases: Consider your business needs and the potential applications your stakeholders and SMEs (subject matter experts) find most promising. Evaluate these against the ease and cost of development. Review applications discussed in our upcoming books, which will detail AI tools' capabilities and

> **Select the Right Tools and Frameworks**
>
> **Power Platform: Review Microsoft's Power Platform and CoPilot to see if that is your best solution. Can these do everything you need and not leave you painted into a corner?**
>
> **.NET Libraries: Leverage .NET libraries like ML.NET, AutoML, Semantic Kernel, and CoPilot for scalable and robust solutions.**
>
> **Cloud Services: Look at what AI services Azure, AWS, and Google offer. How much work do they require to make useful?**

offer free prototype code. These prototypes can be quickly and economically developed with low risk.

2. Develop Multiple Prototypes: For each promising idea, develop a prototype using the code and guidance provided in our future publications.

3. Evaluate Prototypes: Have your AI Innovation Team, particularly stakeholders and SMEs, assess these prototypes to determine their effectiveness and potential.

4. Decide the Future of Each Prototype: Determine which prototypes should be shelved, which need revisions or further development, and which are successful enough to evolve into an MVP.

5. Adjust AI Tools If Necessary: If a prototype needs better functionality, consider switching AI tools. For example, switch to a more robust tool like Microsoft Azure Vision AI or AWS Textract if your current OCR tool underperforms.

6. Define MVP Requirements: The Business Requirements Analyst of the AI Innovation Team should define what essential and basic functions the MVP must have, informed by stakeholder needs and development feasibility. Select functions that offer the greatest value with the least investment.

7. Evaluate the MVP: Once the MVP is developed, it should be evaluated by the AI Innovation Team to decide if it should be stopped, revised, or moved forward to production development.

8. Transition MVP to Production: To promote an MVP to production, stakeholders and SMEs must clearly define the required features, while developers assess the complexity of these features, categorizing them as easy, moderate, or difficult. Consider implementing these features in phases (Phase 1, Phase 2, etc.).

By following these steps, you can streamline the development process from prototype to production, ensuring that each stage is managed effectively with clear objectives and rigorous evaluation to maximize the potential of your AI applications.

Rethinking Development Resources

A critical consideration in your AI journey involves evaluating your development resources. It's essential to think of how consultants can serve as an extension of your development team. Deciding which resources will develop your prototypes and MVPs is key.

Typically, you may have a team dedicated to your regular business applications. Allocating one or more of these developers to prototype development could impact the maintenance and progress of your existing applications.

Consider how many developers you can realistically divert to this new endeavor. Often, the reality is that only one or two can be spared without significant disruption. Could hiring additional developers to support your regular projects be a solution? Additionally, it's worth considering whether your most experienced developers should lead the AI initiatives, keeping in mind that not all developers may be inclined toward new technologies and innovation.

Start with Small Datasets

Sample Data: Begin with a small, manageable dataset to quickly iterate and test your prototype. If the Innovation Team likes the prototype, start expanding both good and bad test cases.

Synthetic Data: Use synthetic data generation techniques if real data is scarce or sensitive.

As an AI application transitions from a prototype to an MVP, decisions need to be made about personnel continuity. Should the same developer who created the prototype also develop the MVP, or is it more efficient for them to start another prototype and pass the ongoing project to someone else? Typically, the original developer would need to provide guidance to whoever takes over the MVP development. This could be an opportunity for a mid-level developer looking to step up into a more senior role.

When an AI application progresses from MVP to production, consider whether this is the appropriate time to integrate your regular business application developers. This stage often involves expanding your regular development team's responsibilities to include turning the MVP into a production-ready product, which could dilute your resource pool.

Long term, the goal should be for your regular developers to manage the ongoing development, new features, bug fixes, and maintenance of the AI applications. Determining the optimal timing and approach for this transition can vary significantly from one business to another.

If you're short on resources, we can help with just training, consulting, coaching. We can also develop prototypes, MVPs, and production ready code—for your use cases and requirements.

Step-by-step Guide to Building an AI Application

Developing an AI prototype involves a series of methodical steps that range from problem definition to deployment. Here's a step-by-step guide to navigating this process effectively:

Step 1: Define the Problem

Start by clearly identifying the problem you aim to solve with AI. This involves understanding the needs of your target users, the specific challenges they face, and how AI can help address these challenges. A well-articulated problem statement will guide the entire development process. Determine your key stakeholder—a department head or manager who is willing to test the prototype and provide feedback.

Step 2: Explore AI Technologies

Learn about the different AI technologies that could solve your problem. Consider whether a low-code solution like Microsoft

CoPilot or Power Tools fits your needs or if a more controlled environment like a Microsoft Visual Studio application in C# or VB.NET would be better.

Remember, C# or VB.NET allows for integration with standard source control, DevOps, and security protocols.

Step 3: Gather and Prepare Data

AI models depend heavily on data to learn and make predictions. Collect relevant data that helps your prototype to understand and analyze the problem. This step may involve compiling new data sets or utilizing existing ones. Once collected, clean and preprocess the data to ensure it is analysis-ready. The nature of the data can vary greatly depending on the application, such as analyzing insurance claims or detecting fraudulent transactions.

> **Rapid Prototyping Techniques**
>
> **Low-Code/No-Code: Use low-code or no-code platforms to quickly build and iterate on your prototype. Be careful—low code / no code can paint you in a corner and take more time than a .NET application.**
>
> **First version of the prototype: Don't think about functionality. Try to get all the components to work together—just to do something—and prove that you can add functionality later.**
>
> **Agile Methodology: Implement agile development practices for rapid iteration and continuous improvement.**

Step 4: Choose the Right AI Model(s)

Select the AI model that best suits your defined problem and data characteristics. Options might include neural networks, decision trees, or clustering algorithms. You may need to experiment with multiple models to identify which one yields the best results. Tools like Microsoft's AutoML can automate this process by testing several models to determine the most effective one.

Step 5: Train the AI Model

Train your chosen AI model by feeding it the prepared data. This step is computationally intensive, and the duration will depend on the model's complexity and the data volume.

Step 6: Evaluate the Model

After training, assess the model's performance using a separate validation dataset. Evaluation metrics might include accuracy, precision, recall, or F1 score, tailored to the specifics of your problem.

Step 7: Iterate and Improve

Refine your model based on evaluation outcomes. This may involve adjusting hyperparameters, enhancing the data set, or employing different modeling techniques. Iteration is vital to optimize the prototype's accuracy and functionality. Present your findings to the AI Innovation Team and your stakeholder for feedback.

Step 8: Integrate and Deploy

Once your model is adequately refined, integrate it into the intended application or system. This could involve developing a user interface, linking the model to other system components, or establishing a deployment environment. Then launch your AI prototype for user interaction and feedback.

Focus on Simplicity

Avoid Over-engineering: Keep the prototype simple and avoid adding unnecessary features.

MVP Approach: Develop a Minimum Viable Product (MVP) that focuses on core functionalities.

Step 9: Monitor and Maintain

Continuously monitor the AI prototype post-deployment to track its performance and gather user feedback. Regular maintenance and updates are crucial to ensure the prototype remains effective and adapts to any new requirements or feedback over time.

Following these steps will help you develop a robust AI prototype, paving the way from a basic concept to a functional tool ready for iterative improvement and eventual deployment.

Navigating Challenges in Innovation: Two Steps Forward, One Step Back

In the realm of innovation and custom product development, encountering a showstopper is often par for the course, whether you're developing an AI application, designing a new car, or building a custom home. In fact, it's more surprising not to run into significant obstacles during these complex and innovative projects.

This commonality is precisely why we emphasize the importance of developing prototypes and MVPs (minimally viable products). The philosophy of "failing early and fast" is critical; it allows teams to identify limitations and critical issues as early as possible. When these showstoppers appear, it's important not to panic. Instead, take a moment to analyze the situation. Consider if there are ways to pivot, adapt, and overcome the challenge. Ask yourself: Do we need different tools? Could we approach the problem differently? Is it possible to bring in external expertise to help surmount this obstacle?

Importantly, encountering a showstopper doesn't necessarily mean starting over from scratch. For example, if you hit a major hurdle in the middle of developing an MVP, you don't need to revert entirely to the prototype phase—though keeping that option on the table is wise. Consider whether you can isolate the issue by developing a new prototype focused solely on that specific problem. Once resolved, this piece can be reintegrated into the broader MVP.

In essence, encountering significant challenges is a natural part of tackling new and innovative projects. When it happens, don't let it derail your progress. Instead, use it as an opportunity to refine your approach and strengthen your final product. Remember, setbacks are not just obstacles; they are also catalysts for growth and improvement.

Additional Considerations for AI Application Development

As your AI application progresses from a prototype to an MVP and eventually to a production-ready product, integrating it into your standard operational frameworks becomes crucial.

This includes your source code repository, DevOps processes, testing protocols, and security frameworks. While these elements may not be critical during the prototype phase, they become essential as you move toward a production environment.

> **Iterate and Improve**
>
> **Continuous Feedback: Gather feedback from stakeholders and end-users to refine the prototype.**
>
> **After a successful minimally viable product, hand application off to a regular software development team to make production ready.**

It's advantageous to develop your AI application as a library. This approach provides flexibility regardless of the final application format, whether it be a console application, mobile app, website, web API service, or even a containerized application designed for platforms like AWS Fargate or Azure Container Instances.

When using C# or VB.NET, it doesn't matter if you're deploying on Windows or Linux servers—developing your AI application as a library allows for such versatility. Our philosophy is centered on flexibility: By developing your AI application as a library, you can later adapt it to any front-end interface required by different user groups. For instance, one group might need the AI application integrated into a website, another might require it as a web API service, and yet another might opt for containerized deployment. This method ensures that your AI application can meet diverse needs and usage scenarios efficiently.

Do You Find the Book Too Simple?

If you find this book too simple or focused on common sense, we recommend exploring more advanced topics. Look for books and YouTube videos that combine AI, machine learning (ML), statistics, mathematics, operations research, linear algebra, and programming. Additionally, search for .NET libraries that perform these functions and experiment with them. You might be surprised by how much AI and ML you can achieve using these libraries. You may need to convert some code from Python to C# or VB.NET, but many popular Python libraries, like SymPy, NumPy, and Scikit-learn, have .NET equivalents.

Books

The StatQuest Illustrated Guide To Machine Learning by Josh Starmer

Essential Math for Data Science: Take Control of Your Data with Fundamental Linear Algebra, Probability, and Statistics by Thomas Nield

Practical Statistics for Data Scientists. 50+ Essential Concepts using R and Python by Peter Bruce, Andrew Bruce, and Peter Gedeck

YouTube Channels:

StatQuest with Josh Starmer

3Blue1Brown

Chapter 6:
Leveraging Microsoft and other Technologies

Introduction

In this chapter, we delve into an extensive range of AI technologies and platforms, with a particular emphasis on Microsoft's offerings alongside other leading providers in the industry. As businesses increasingly look to incorporate AI into their operations, understanding the capabilities and potential applications of these technologies is essential.

We start with an overview of Microsoft's suite of low code/no code tools, which are designed to enable businesses to analyze data, build solutions, automate processes, and create virtual agents. Although marketed as user-friendly and not necessarily requiring a developer, the reality is that while these tools are quick and cost-effective, they may not always deliver the depth required for more complex applications. They are ideal for simple AI tasks and can be the most efficient choice for straightforward projects.

We also examine OpenAI, renowned for its cutting-edge natural language processing models. OpenAI operates independently but has strategic partnerships with Microsoft that enhance integration and accessibility.

Our discussion extends to Visual Studio tools like Semantic Kernel, ML.NET, AutoML, TorchSharp, and SciSharp, which provide robust capabilities for machine learning and AI development. We evaluate their practical applications and integration into business processes.

For those with access to Visual Studio developers, these tools might offer the best value. They allow for a broad range of functionalities at a slightly higher cost than Microsoft's low code options but do not support training of large AI models.

For heavy-duty AI tasks, cloud platforms like Azure, AWS, Google, or IBM are more suitable. Azure AI tools often provide superior capabilities compared to Visual Studio-based tools. By using a Visual Studio application, you can leverage Azure AI services for intensive tasks while handling routine workflow with your C# or VB.NET applications. .NET applications can also integrate services from AWS, Google, and IBM.

> "Data is the new oil. It's valuable, but if unrefined it cannot really be used. It has to be changed into gas, plastic, chemicals, etc. to create a valuable entity that drives profitable activity; so must data be broken down, analyzed for it to have value."
>
> - Clive Humby

Additionally, we explore Microsoft's Open Neural Network Exchange, a platform that promotes the sharing and deployment of AI models across various frameworks and tools.

We also cover the advanced AI tools and services available in Azure AI and provide an overview of AI services offered by AWS, Google, and IBM. These sections aim to equip you with a comprehensive understanding of the available technologies and their potential to enhance business operations.

By the end of this chapter, you will have a solid foundation in the diverse range of AI technologies and platforms available, enabling you to make informed decisions about which tools are best suited to your business needs and how they can be effectively leveraged for innovation and growth.

Overview of Microsoft AI Tools and Platforms

Microsoft has a range of tools for businesses wanting to use AI. We typically break them into low/no code, Visual Studio (C# or VB.NET) applications, and Azure AI services.

Overview of Microsoft Power Platform

Microsoft Power Platform is a suite of tools designed to empower organizations to analyze data, automate workflows, build applications, and create virtual agents, all with minimal coding. It consists of four main components: Power BI, Power Apps, Power Automate, and Power Virtual Agents. Together, these tools provide a comprehensive solution for business intelligence, app development, process automation, and chatbot creation.

Power BI

Tools: Power BI Desktop, Power BI Service, Power BI Mobile

Use Cases:

- Data visualization and dashboards
- Business performance tracking
- Insights and analytics for decision-making

Applications:

- Financial reporting

- Sales and marketing analysis
- Supply chain optimization

Power Apps

Tools: Canvas apps, Model-driven apps, Portals

Use Cases:

- Custom business app development
- Mobile app creation for field services
- Internal process automation

Applications:

- Employee onboarding apps
- Customer service portals
- Inventory management systems

Power Automate

Tools: Cloud flows, Desktop flows, Business process flows

Use Cases:

- Workflow automation
- Data integration between systems
- Task scheduling and reminders

> "The goal of AI is to make systems that are less mechanical and more intelligent, more like a human and less like a computer."
>
> - Geoffrey Hinton

Applications:

- Automated approval processes
- Synchronization of data across platforms
- Streamlining repetitive tasks

Power Virtual Agents

Tools: Chatbot builder, AI-driven suggestions, Integration with Power Automate

Use Cases:

- Customer support chatbots
- Internal helpdesk automation
- FAQ bots for websites

Applications:

- Reducing customer service response times
- Providing 24/7 support
- Guiding users through processes or services

The Microsoft Power Platform enables businesses to harness the power of data and AI without the need for extensive technical expertise. By leveraging these tools, organizations can streamline operations, enhance decision-making, and improve customer experiences.

Overview of Microsoft Copilot

Microsoft Copilot is an AI-powered assistant designed to enhance productivity and creativity across various Microsoft applications. It leverages advanced natural language processing and machine learning technologies to provide users with intelligent suggestions, automation, and insights.

Tools

Copilot in Word: Assists with writing, editing, and formatting documents.

Copilot in Excel: Provides data analysis, insights, and visualization recommendations.

Copilot in PowerPoint: Helps create engaging presentations with design suggestions and content ideas.

Copilot in Outlook: Assists with email drafting, scheduling, and task management.

Use Cases

Content Creation: Copilot can generate text, suggest edits, and help structure documents in Word, making it easier to create high-quality content quickly.

Data Analysis: In Excel, Copilot can analyze data, suggest trends, and create visualizations, enabling users to gain insights from their data without deep expertise in data analysis.

> "The opportunities we can take advantage of by leveraging AI are staggering. Innovations in AI will enable us to solve problems today that were once considered impossible to solve."
>
> - Fei-Fei Li

Presentation Design: Copilot in PowerPoint can suggest design layouts, provide content ideas, and help users create professional-looking presentations with minimal effort.

Email Management: In Outlook, Copilot can draft emails, suggest responses, and help manage calendars, streamlining communication and scheduling tasks.

Applications

Business Reports: Copilot can assist in drafting and formatting business reports, ensuring clarity and consistency in presentation.

Market Analysis: Users can leverage Copilot in Excel to analyze market trends, forecast sales, and visualize data for informed decision-making.

Training Materials: Copilot in PowerPoint can help create engaging training materials, incorporating relevant content and visual aids.

Customer Communication: Copilot can help draft personalized emails and responses to customer inquiries, improving efficiency and customer satisfaction.

Microsoft Copilot is a versatile tool that integrates seamlessly with familiar Microsoft applications, enhancing productivity and enabling users to focus on higher-value tasks. By leveraging AI, Copilot assists users in various aspects of their work, from content creation to data analysis, making it an invaluable asset in the modern workplace.

Overview of OpenAI

OpenAI is a research organization and technology company focused on developing artificial intelligence in a safe and beneficial manner. It is known for its cutting-edge advancements in natural language processing, machine learning, and generative AI technologies. OpenAI's tools and models have a wide range of applications across various industries. Microsoft and OpenAI are partners and have a lot of close collaboration.

> "AI is the new electricity. Just as electricity transformed almost everything 100 years ago, today I actually have a hard time thinking of an industry that I don't think AI will transform in the next several years."
>
> - Andrew Ng

Tools

GPT-4 (Generative Pre-trained Transformer 4): A state-of-the-art language processing AI model capable of generating human-like text, answering questions, translating languages, and more.

DALL-E: An AI model that generates images from textual descriptions, enabling creative and design applications.

Codex: A model that translates natural language into code, assisting in software development and automation tasks.

Use Cases

Content Generation: GPT-4 can create articles, blog posts, and marketing content, reducing the time and effort required for content creation.

Customer Support: Integration of GPT-4 into chatbots and virtual assistants enhances customer service with more natural and context-aware responses.

Language Translation: GPT-4's ability to understand and translate multiple languages can facilitate global communication and content localization.

Creative Design: DALL-E can generate unique images and designs based on textual descriptions, offering new possibilities for graphic design and branding.

Applications

Automated Writing Assistants: GPT-4-powered tools can assist writers in generating ideas, editing text, and improving the quality of written content.

E-commerce: Chatbots enhanced with GPT-4 can provide personalized shopping experiences, product recommendations, and customer support.

Education: GPT-4 can be used to create interactive learning materials, generate quiz questions, and provide explanations for complex concepts.

Software Development: Codex can help developers write code more efficiently by translating natural language instructions into programming code.

OpenAI's technologies have the potential to revolutionize how businesses operate, offering innovative solutions for content creation, customer engagement, and automation. By leveraging these tools, organizations can stay ahead in the rapidly evolving landscape of AI.

Overview of Microsoft Semantic Kernel

Microsoft Semantic Kernel is a cutting-edge AI technology that enables sophisticated understanding and processing of natural language. It is designed to enhance a wide range of applications, from search engines to content analysis tools, by providing deep semantic insights into text.

Tools

Language Models: Advanced machine learning models trained on vast amounts of text data to understand and generate human-like language.

Text Analytics: Tools for extracting meaning, sentiment, and key phrases from text, enabling more nuanced analysis and categorization.

> "The true promise of AI is not about making something that thinks like a human, but in creating a new kind of intelligence that complements and enhances our own." - Nick Bostrom

Semantic Search: Enhanced search capabilities that understand the intent and context of queries, providing more relevant and accurate results.

Use Cases

Content Recommendation: Semantic Kernel can analyze user preferences and content characteristics to deliver personalized recommendations in streaming platforms, news aggregators, and e-commerce sites.

Sentiment Analysis: In customer feedback or social media monitoring, Semantic Kernel can determine the sentiment of text, helping businesses understand customer opinions and trends.

Document Clustering: For organizing large document collections, Semantic Kernel can group documents based on their semantic similarity, aiding in information retrieval and knowledge management.

Applications

Search Engines: Integrating Semantic Kernel into search engines enhances their ability to understand and respond to complex queries, providing users with more relevant search results.

Content Management Systems: Semantic Kernel can assist in automatically categorizing and tagging content, streamlining content management processes.

Customer Support: In chatbots and virtual assistants, Semantic Kernel can improve natural language understanding, enabling more effective and human-like interactions with users.

Microsoft Semantic Kernel represents a significant advancement in natural language processing, offering powerful tools for understanding and leveraging the complexities of human language in a wide range of applications.

Integration of Microsoft Semantic Kernel with OpenAI APIs

Microsoft Semantic Kernel can be integrated with OpenAI APIs to enhance its capabilities and leverage the strengths of both technologies. OpenAI provides a range of APIs for natural language processing, including the powerful GPT models, which can complement the semantic understanding provided by Semantic Kernel.

Integration Process

API Setup: To integrate Semantic Kernel with OpenAI, developers first need to set up access to OpenAI APIs by obtaining an API key and configuring the necessary endpoints.

> "The only way to predict the future is to have the power to shape it."
>
> **Eric Hoffer**

Data Preprocessing: Before sending text data to OpenAI APIs, Semantic Kernel can preprocess the data to extract key semantic features and context.

API Calls: The preprocessed data is then sent to OpenAI APIs for further analysis, such as language generation, text completion, or semantic search.

Combining Results: The responses from OpenAI APIs are combined with the semantic insights from Semantic Kernel to create enriched outputs that leverage the strengths of both technologies.

Use Cases

Enhanced Chatbots: By integrating Semantic Kernel with OpenAI's GPT models, chatbots can achieve a deeper understanding of user queries and generate more contextually relevant responses.

Advanced Text Analysis: Combining Semantic Kernel's ability to extract semantic meaning with OpenAI's language models can result in more sophisticated text analysis tools that can understand nuances and complex concepts.

Improved Content Recommendations: Integrating these technologies can lead to better content recommendation engines that consider both semantic relevance and user preferences.

Applications

Customer Service: Integration can improve customer service platforms by enabling more accurate and context-aware responses to customer inquiries.

Research and Development: In R&D, this integration can enhance literature review and analysis tools, helping researchers find and understand relevant information more efficiently.

Content Creation: For content creators, combining Semantic Kernel and OpenAI APIs can assist in generating ideas, summarizing information, and creating content that is semantically rich and engaging.

By integrating Microsoft Semantic Kernel with OpenAI APIs, developers can create applications that benefit from advanced natural language understanding, combining semantic insights with the generative and analytical capabilities of OpenAI's models.

Overview of Microsoft ML.NET

Microsoft ML.NET is an open-source, cross-platform machine learning framework designed specifically for .NET developers. It allows for the creation and integration of custom machine learning models into .NET applications, enabling developers to add AI capabilities without needing extensive machine learning expertise.

> **"The power of AI is in its ability to learn and adapt, turning data into actionable insights."**
>
> **-Anonymous**

Tools

Model Builder: A visual interface in Visual Studio that simplifies the process of building and training machine learning models.

CLI (Command-Line Interface): For developers who prefer working in a command-line environment, ML.NET offers a CLI tool for model training and evaluation.

AutoML: An automated machine learning feature that selects the best algorithm and hyperparameters for your data, simplifying model development.

Use Cases

Sentiment Analysis: ML.NET can be used to analyze customer reviews or social media posts to determine the sentiment (positive, negative, neutral) of the text.

Product Recommendation: Retailers can leverage ML.NET to create personalized product recommendation systems based on customer purchase history and preferences.

Fraud Detection: Financial institutions can use ML.NET to build models that detect fraudulent transactions by analyzing patterns in transaction data.

Applications

Health care: ML.NET can be applied in health care for predictive analytics, such as forecasting patient readmission risks or identifying potential health issues from medical records.

Manufacturing: In the manufacturing sector, ML.NET can be used for predictive maintenance, analyzing sensor data to predict equipment failures and schedule maintenance proactively.

Customer Service: ML.NET can enhance customer service by enabling chatbots and virtual assistants to understand and respond to customer queries more effectively.

ML.NET offers a versatile and accessible approach to integrating machine learning into .NET applications, empowering developers to create intelligent, data-driven solutions across various industries.

Overview of Microsoft AutoML

Microsoft AutoML, part of the Visual Studio and Azure Machine Learning platform, is an automated machine learning tool that simplifies the process of building, training, and deploying machine learning models. It is designed to automate the selection of the best machine learning algorithms and hyperparameters for a given dataset and task, making machine learning more accessible to non-experts.

Think of AutoML as another Microsoft low code/no code way of developing AI.

Tools

Azure Machine Learning Studio: A web-based interface for managing AutoML experiments, training models, and deploying solutions.

Azure ML SDK: A software development kit for integrating AutoML into custom applications and workflows.

Use Cases

Predictive Maintenance: AutoML can be used to build models that predict equipment failures, helping businesses schedule maintenance and avoid downtime.

Customer Churn Prediction: Companies can use AutoML to identify patterns in customer behavior that indicate a risk of churn, enabling targeted retention strategies.

Sales Forecasting: AutoML can assist in developing models that forecast sales, helping businesses plan inventory and optimize pricing strategies.

Applications

Financial Services: In banking and finance, AutoML can be used for credit scoring, fraud detection, and risk assessment, improving decision-making and reducing losses.

Health care: AutoML can help in developing predictive models for patient outcomes, treatment effectiveness, and disease progression, enhancing patient care and operational efficiency.

Retail: Retailers can leverage AutoML for demand forecasting, personalized marketing, and customer segmentation, driving sales and improving customer experiences.

Microsoft AutoML democratizes machine learning by automating complex tasks and enabling businesses to harness the power of AI without requiring deep expertise in data science. This tool empowers organizations to innovate and optimize their operations with data-driven insights.

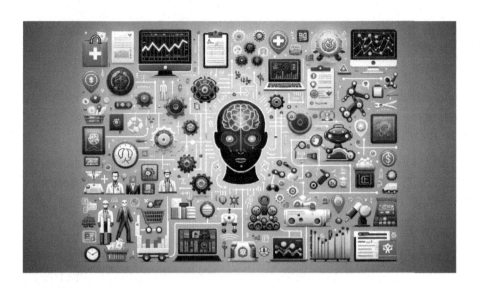

Overview of Microsoft AutoGen (Multi-agent Conversation Framework)

Microsoft AutoGen is a multi-agent conversation framework designed to facilitate the development of conversational AI systems. It enables the creation of sophisticated dialogue systems that can handle multiple participants and complex conversational flows.

Tools

Dialogue Management: AutoGen provides tools for managing dialogue states, transitions, and interactions between multiple agents.

Natural Language Understanding (NLU): The framework includes NLU components for interpreting user inputs and extracting relevant information.

Natural Language Generation (NLG): AutoGen offers NLG capabilities for generating coherent and contextually appropriate responses.

Use Cases

Customer Service Chatbots: AutoGen can be used to develop chatbots that can handle multi-turn conversations and engage with multiple users simultaneously, providing efficient customer support.

Collaborative Virtual Assistants: The framework can facilitate the creation of virtual assistants that coordinate tasks and information between different users and systems.

Interactive Training Simulations: AutoGen is suitable for developing training simulations where participants interact with AI agents in role-playing scenarios to learn and practice skills.

Applications

E-commerce: In e-commerce platforms, AutoGen can power chatbots that assist customers in finding products, answering queries, and facilitating transactions.

Health care: The framework can be used to create virtual health assistants that interact with patients, health care providers, and medical systems to coordinate care and provide information.

Education: AutoGen can enable the development of educational chatbots that facilitate collaborative learning, tutoring, and interactive coursework.

Microsoft AutoGen's multi-agent conversation framework offers a robust foundation for building advanced conversational AI systems that can handle complex interactions and provide engaging user experiences. By leveraging AutoGen, developers can create AI agents that communicate effectively with users and other agents, enhancing the capabilities of conversational interfaces across various domains.

Overview of Microsoft TorchSharp and SciSharp

Microsoft TorchSharp and SciSharp are open-source libraries that bring the power of deep learning and scientific computing to the .NET ecosystem. TorchSharp is a .NET binding for the popular

PyTorch library, while SciSharp provides .NET bindings for various scientific computing libraries, including TensorFlow and NumPy.

TorchSharp

Tools:

TorchTensor: Represents multidimensional arrays and provides tensor operations.

TorchNN: Contains neural network modules and functions for building deep learning models.

> **"Integrating AI into your business isn't just about adopting technology; it's about transforming your approach to problem-solving."**

TorchOptim: Includes optimization algorithms for training models.

Use Cases:

Image Classification: Building and training convolutional neural networks (CNNs) for classifying images.

Natural Language Processing: Developing recurrent neural networks (RNNs) or transformers for text analysis and language modeling.

Generative Models: Creating generative adversarial networks (GANs) or variational autoencoders (VAEs) for generating new data samples.

Applications:

Medical Imaging: Analyzing medical images for diagnosis and treatment planning.

Sentiment Analysis: Processing customer reviews or social media posts to determine sentiment.

Anomaly Detection: Identifying unusual patterns or outliers in data for fraud detection or quality control.

SciSharp

Tools:

TensorFlow.NET: A .NET binding for TensorFlow, allowing for the creation and training of machine learning models.

NumSharp: A library similar to NumPy, providing support for large, multi-dimensional arrays and matrices.

Pandas.NET: Inspired by the panda's library, it offers data manipulation and analysis features.

Use Cases:

Predictive Modeling: Using TensorFlow.NET to build and train models for forecasting and prediction.

Data Analysis: Employing NumSharp and Pandas.NET for data cleaning, transformation, and exploration.

Scientific Computing: Applying mathematical and statistical methods to solve scientific problems.

Applications:

Financial Forecasting: Developing models to predict stock prices or market trends.

Bioinformatics: Analyzing biological data for research and development in health care.

Environmental Modeling: Creating simulations to study climate change or natural resource management.

> "The future of AI is not just about building smarter machines, but about creating systems that understand and enhance human capabilities."
>
> - Anonymous

Microsoft TorchSharp and SciSharp provide .NET developers with powerful tools for deep learning and scientific computing, enabling them to leverage the capabilities of popular Python libraries within the .NET environment. These libraries open up new possibilities for building advanced AI applications across various domains.

Overview of Microsoft Open Neural Network Exchanges (ONNX)

Microsoft Open Neural Network Exchange (ONNX) is an open-source format for representing machine learning models. ONNX provides a common framework for interoperability between different AI frameworks and tools, allowing developers to easily transfer models across platforms and optimize them for various hardware devices.

Tools

ONNX Runtime: A high-performance inference engine that optimizes and runs ONNX models on various hardware platforms, including CPUs, GPUs, and edge devices.

ONNX Converter: A set of tools and libraries that convert models from popular frameworks like PyTorch, TensorFlow, and Keras into the ONNX format.

Use Cases

Model Portability: ONNX enables the transfer of models between different frameworks, allowing developers to choose the best tools for training and deployment.

Model Optimization: The ONNX Runtime optimizes models for specific hardware, improving performance and efficiency in deployment.

Edge Computing: ONNX models can be deployed on edge devices for real-time inference, making it suitable for applications like IoT and autonomous vehicles.

Applications

Computer Vision: ONNX models can be used for tasks such as object detection, image classification, and facial recognition in security systems, retail analytics, and autonomous vehicles.

Natural Language Processing: ONNX supports models for language translation, sentiment analysis, and chatbots, enhancing customer service and communication platforms.

Predictive Maintenance: In manufacturing, ONNX models can analyze sensor data to predict equipment failures and schedule maintenance, reducing downtime and costs.

> "Building AI systems is as much an art as it is a science. It requires a blend of technical skills, creativity, and an understanding of the human experience."
>
> - Kai-Fu Lee

Microsoft's Open Neural Network Exchange (ONNX) simplifies the deployment of AI models across diverse environments, making it easier for businesses to leverage the power of AI in their applications. By providing a common format and runtime for models, ONNX enables greater flexibility and efficiency in AI development and deployment.

Overview of Non Microsoft AI tools and platforms

While Microsoft offers a comprehensive suite of AI tools and platforms, there are numerous non-Microsoft AI technologies that businesses can leverage to meet their specific needs. These tools provide a wide range of capabilities, from machine learning and deep learning to natural language processing and computer vision. Although integrating non-Microsoft AI tools into your technology stack may increase the learning curve, the availability of software development kits (SDKs) and application programming interfaces (APIs) makes it easier to interface with these technologies.

By utilizing SDKs and APIs, businesses can seamlessly integrate these non-Microsoft AI tools into their existing Microsoft technology stack, expanding their AI capabilities and enabling more sophisticated solutions. The key is to choose the right tools based on the specific requirements of your AI projects and ensure that your team has the necessary skills to work with these technologies effectively.

It's not uncommon for a business to use AWS, Google, or IBM AI services. It's not uncommon for a Microsoft Visual Studio (C# or VB.NET) application to call AI services in AWS, Google AI, and IBM AI. If your business is built on the Microsoft technology stack and you need to use AWS, Google, or IBM AI Services, instead of developing the AI application entirely on AWS, Google, or IBM, you develop the AI application using visual studio and simply call AWS, Google, or IBM using SDKs and APIs. This way, you reduce costs, risk, less learning, use your existing source control, DevOps, testing, and security.

Overview of AWS AI Services

Amazon Web Services (AWS) offers a comprehensive suite of AI services that enable businesses to build intelligent applications and solutions. These services leverage machine learning, natural language processing, and computer vision technologies to provide capabilities that range from text and speech analysis to image and video recognition.

Amazon SageMaker

Tools: SageMaker is a fully managed service that provides every developer and data scientist with the ability to build, train, and deploy machine learning models quickly.

Use Cases: SageMaker is used for a wide range of machine learning tasks, including predictive modeling, natural language processing, and recommendation systems.

Applications: It is commonly used in health care for patient outcome prediction, in retail for personalized recommendations, and in finance for fraud detection.

Amazon Lex

Tools: Lex is a service for building conversational interfaces using voice and text, powered by the same technology as Alexa.

Use Cases: Lex is used to create chatbots for customer service, virtual assistants for productivity, and conversational agents for various applications.

Applications: It is used in banking for customer support chatbots, in hospitality for booking assistants, and in health care for patient engagement.

Amazon Rekognition

Tools: Rekognition is a service that makes it easy to add image and video analysis to your applications.

Use Cases: Rekognition is used for image and video recognition tasks, such as facial recognition, object detection, and content moderation.

Applications: It is used in security for surveillance systems, in media for content categorization, and in retail for customer engagement through visual search.

Amazon Comprehend

Tools: Comprehend is a natural language processing (NLP) service that uses machine learning to uncover insights and relationships in text.

Use Cases: Comprehend is used for sentiment analysis, entity recognition, and text classification.

Applications: It is used in social media monitoring for sentiment analysis, in customer feedback analysis for understanding customer sentiment, and in content management for automatic tagging and organization.

Amazon Translate

Tools: Translate is a neural machine translation service that delivers fast, high-quality, and affordable language translation.

Use Cases: Translate is used for real-time text translation in multiple languages, supporting applications like multilingual content creation and global communication.

Applications: It is used in e-commerce for product descriptions translation, in customer support for multilingual chatbots, and in content localization for global audiences.

AWS AI Services provide a wide range of tools that enable businesses to add intelligence to their applications without requiring deep expertise in machine learning or AI. By leveraging these services, companies can improve customer experiences, automate processes, and gain insights from their data.

AWS has made integrating its AI services with C# and VB.NET applications straightforward through its SDKs and Visual Studio extensions. These tools provide an efficient development experience, enabling .NET developers to easily utilize AWS's powerful AI services.

The AWS SDK for .NET offers libraries for connecting to various AWS AI services like Amazon Rekognition, Amazon Polly, and Amazon Comprehend. These libraries simplify adding AI capabilities to applications by handling the complexities of API interactions.

AWS also offers the AWS Toolkit for Visual Studio, which integrates directly into the IDE. This toolkit provides features that simplify developing, debugging, and deploying .NET applications using AWS services. Developers can access and manage AWS resources directly from Visual Studio, speeding up the development process.

One major benefit of these tools is the minimal configuration needed to use AWS AI services. For example, setting up Amazon Rekognition can be quickly done through the Visual Studio extension, which guides developers in configuring AWS credentials and permissions.

Additionally, the AWS SDK for .NET and Visual Studio extensions support best practices in security and performance. They include built-in support for authentication, encryption, and error management, ensuring high standards of security and reliability. Performance monitoring and debugging tools help optimize applications for speed and cost-efficiency.

Overview of Google AI Services

Google AI services offer a broad range of tools and platforms that enable businesses to incorporate advanced artificial intelligence capabilities into their applications. These services leverage Google's expertise in machine learning, natural language processing, and computer vision to provide scalable and accessible solutions for a variety of use cases.

Google Cloud AI Platform

Tools: The AI Platform is a comprehensive suite for building, training, and deploying machine learning models at scale. It includes tools for data preprocessing, model development, hyperparameter tuning, and model serving.

Use Cases: The AI Platform is used for developing custom machine learning models for tasks such as predictive analytics, classification, and regression analysis.

Applications: It is commonly used in industries like finance for risk assessment, health care for disease prediction, and retail for demand forecasting.

Google Cloud Natural Language

Tools: This service provides natural language understanding capabilities, including sentiment analysis, entity recognition, and syntax analysis.

Use Cases: Cloud Natural Language is used for extracting insights and metadata from text, enabling applications to understand human language.

Applications: It is used in customer feedback analysis, content categorization, and chatbot development for more intuitive interactions.

Google Cloud Vision

Tools: Cloud Vision is a service that allows developers to integrate image recognition and analysis into their applications.

Use Cases: Cloud Vision is used for tasks such as object detection, facial recognition, and optical character recognition (OCR).

Applications: It is used in security for surveillance systems, in retail for product identification, and in document management for digitizing and indexing printed documents.

Google Cloud Speech-to-Text and Text-to-Speech

Tools: These services convert audio to text and text to audio, respectively, using advanced neural network models.

Use Cases: Speech-to-text is used for transcribing audio content, while Text-to-Speech is used for generating natural-sounding speech from text.

Applications: They are used in virtual assistants, voice-enabled applications, and accessibility tools for people with disabilities.

Google Cloud Translation

Tools: This service provides real-time translation capabilities for over 100 languages.

Use Cases: Cloud Translation is used for translating text and websites into different languages, enabling global communication and content localization.

Applications: It is used in e-commerce for translating product descriptions, in customer support for multilingual interactions, and in content management for reaching a wider audience.

Google AI services offer powerful tools for integrating AI into various applications, enabling businesses to leverage Google's cutting-edge technology to enhance their services, automate processes, and gain insights from data.

Google has streamlined the integration of its cloud services into .NET applications through tools like Google Cloud Tools for Visual Studio and the Google API Client Library for .NET.

Google Cloud Tools for Visual Studio is a robust extension that allows developers to deploy and manage their applications on Google Cloud Platform (GCP) directly from Visual Studio. It supports building and deploying .NET applications to various GCP services, including Google Compute Engine, Google App Engine, and Google Kubernetes Engine. This toolset includes features such as browsing Stackdriver log entries, error reports, and adding remote debugging support for Windows VMs on Google Compute Engine. Additionally, it provides project templates and wizards to simplify the creation of Google Cloud projects, supporting both ASP.NET 4.x and ASP.NET Core runtimes.

Google API Client Library for .NET: enables developers to access a wide range of Google APIs, including Google Drive, YouTube, Calendar, and Analytics. This library supports OAuth 2.0 authentication and offers strongly-typed per-API libraries generated using Google's Discovery API. It is compatible with .NET Framework 4.6.2+, .NET Standard 2.0, and .NET 6.0+, ensuring broad applicability across different .NET environments. Although the library is in maintenance mode, it continues to receive essential updates and bug fixes.

Together, these tools and libraries facilitate a seamless and efficient development experience for .NET developers working with Google Cloud services.

Conclusion

Chapter 6 provides an overview of the diverse array of AI tools and platforms available from Microsoft, as well as a glimpse into the offerings of other major players like AWS and Google. Microsoft's suite of AI tools is extensive, catering to a wide range of applications and use cases. From Power Platform to Semantic Kernel, and from ML.NET to AutoML, Microsoft's AI ecosystem is designed to empower businesses to harness the power of artificial intelligence in various ways.

However, the landscape of AI services is not limited to a single provider. In the real world, businesses often need to leverage the strengths of different platforms to meet their unique requirements. AWS and Google AI services offer robust alternatives and complementary capabilities to Microsoft's offerings. Whether it's the comprehensive machine learning solutions of AWS SageMaker or the powerful natural language processing of Google Cloud Natural Language, these platforms provide valuable tools for businesses looking to integrate AI into their operations.

One of the key advantages of Microsoft's application development environment is its flexibility and interoperability. It is relatively straightforward to call AWS or Google AI services from a C# or VB.NET application, allowing businesses to seamlessly integrate a diverse range of AI capabilities into their Microsoft-based solutions. This flexibility ensures that businesses are not confined to a single ecosystem and can choose the best tools for their specific needs, regardless of the provider.

In conclusion, while Microsoft offers a vast array of AI tools that can be utilized in many different ways, businesses are not limited to a single platform. The reality is that Azure, AWS, and Google all offer similar and competing AI services. The choice of which platform or combination of platforms to use depends on the specific requirements and goals of your business. The key is to understand the strengths and capabilities of each platform and leverage them effectively to drive innovation and success in your AI initiatives.

Chapter 7:
Navigating the AI Landscape

In this chapter, we venture into the broader landscape of artificial intelligence, exploring the various tools, platforms, and strategies that businesses can employ to navigate the complexities of AI adoption. As the AI ecosystem continues to evolve, it's essential for organizations to stay informed about the latest developments and understand how to make strategic choices that align with their goals.

We'll delve into the considerations for selecting AI technologies, balancing the trade-offs between cost, risk, and benefits. You'll learn how to assess the suitability of different AI tools for your specific business problems and how to approach the integration of AI into your existing systems and workflows.

Additionally, we'll discuss the importance of staying updated with AI trends and innovations, and how to foster a culture of continuous learning and adaptation within your organization. By the end of this chapter, you'll be equipped with the knowledge and insights needed to effectively navigate the ever-changing AI landscape and harness the potential of AI to drive your business forward.

Choosing the right AI tools and platforms

Selecting the appropriate AI tools and platforms is crucial for the successful implementation of AI in your business. The right choice can accelerate innovation, enhance efficiency, and provide a competitive edge. Here are key considerations to guide your selection process:

Alignment with Business Objectives

Ensure that the AI tools you choose directly contribute to achieving your specific business goals, whether it's improving customer service, optimizing operations, or driving sales.

Functionality

Evaluate the features and capabilities of the AI tools to ensure they meet your requirements. Look for tools that offer the specific functionalities you need, such as predictive analytics, natural language processing, or image recognition.

Ease of Integration

Consider how easily the AI tools can be integrated into your existing technology stack and workflows. Seamless integration minimizes disruption and speeds up the adoption process.

Scalability

Select AI platforms that can scale with your business needs. As your data volume and processing requirements grow, your AI solutions should be able to handle the increased load efficiently.

User-Friendliness

Opt for tools with intuitive interfaces and comprehensive documentation. This ensures that your team can effectively utilize the AI capabilities without steep learning curves.

> "Machine learning will automate jobs that most people thought could only be done by people."
>
> **Dave Waters**

Customization and Flexibility

Look for AI platforms that offer customization options to tailor the solutions to your specific use cases and industry requirements.

Security and Compliance

Ensure that the AI tools comply with industry standards and regulations, especially regarding data privacy and security.

Cost-Effectiveness

Evaluate the total cost of ownership, including licensing fees, infrastructure costs, and maintenance expenses. Consider the return on investment and choose tools that offer the best value for your budget.

Community and Support

Assess the level of community support and the availability of resources such as forums, tutorials, and customer service. A strong community can provide valuable insights and assistance.

Vendor Reputation and Reliability

Research the reputation of the AI tool vendors. Established vendors with a track record of reliability and innovation are generally preferable.

Performance and Accuracy

Test the performance and accuracy of the AI tools for your specific use cases. High accuracy and fast processing times are critical for effective AI applications.

Extra or New Resources Required

Consider the additional resources that may be required to implement and maintain the AI tools, such as hardware upgrades, specialized personnel, or training programs. Ensure that your organization is prepared to invest in these resources to fully leverage the potential of the AI solutions.

By carefully considering these factors, businesses can select the AI tools and platforms that best align with their objectives, technical capabilities, and budget, ensuring a successful and sustainable AI implementation.

Balancing cost, risk, and benefits in AI adoption

Adopting AI in your business involves careful consideration of the costs, risks, and benefits associated with the technology. Striking the right balance between these factors is crucial for achieving a successful and sustainable AI implementation.

> "In the world of AI, data is king, but context is the kingdom."

Cost

Initial Investment: AI adoption requires an upfront investment in technology, infrastructure, training, and talent. Evaluate the total cost of ownership, including software licenses, hardware, and training expenses.

Maintenance and Upgrades: Consider the ongoing costs of maintaining and updating AI systems to keep them performing optimally and securely.

Cost Savings: Assess the potential cost savings AI can bring through automation, improved efficiency, and reduced errors.

Risk

Data Privacy and Security: Implementing AI involves handling sensitive data, which raises concerns about privacy and security. Ensure that your AI solutions comply with relevant regulations and industry standards.

Implementation Challenges: Be aware of the risks associated with integrating AI into existing systems, including potential technical difficulties and disruptions to workflows.

Adoption Resistance: Consider the risk of resistance from employees or stakeholders who may be skeptical about the changes AI brings. Effective communication and training can mitigate this risk.

Benefits

Competitive Advantage: AI can provide a competitive edge by enabling innovative products and services, personalized customer experiences, and data-driven decision-making.

Operational Efficiency: AI can automate routine tasks, freeing up human resources for more strategic activities and improving overall efficiency.

Data Insights: AI technologies can analyze vast amounts of data to uncover insights that can inform business strategies and drive growth.

Balancing Act

Cost-Benefit Analysis: Conduct a thorough cost-benefit analysis to weigh the financial investment against the expected returns. This analysis should consider both short-term and long-term impacts.

Risk Management: Develop a risk management plan that addresses potential challenges and outlines strategies for mitigating risks. This plan should include regular monitoring and evaluation of the AI implementation.

Iterative Approach: Consider adopting an iterative approach to AI implementation, starting with small-scale projects to demonstrate value and learn from experience before scaling up.

Balancing the cost, risk, and benefits of AI adoption is an ongoing process that requires careful planning, transparent communication, and continuous monitoring. By taking a strategic approach, businesses can maximize the potential of AI while minimizing the associated risks and costs.

Use agile methodologies

It's challenging to define all requirements upfront before a contract starts and for those requirements to remain unchanged throughout the project as new information is learned. Change orders can be prohibitively expensive.

Assuming you have several AI projects ongoing simultaneously, an agile methodology allows you to pause one project to emphasize a more critical one. This approach reduces costs and risks while increasing benefits.

Staying updated with AI trends and innovations

In the rapidly evolving field of artificial intelligence, staying informed about the latest trends and innovations is crucial for businesses looking to leverage AI effectively. Here are some strategies to keep abreast of developments in AI:

Follow Industry Leaders and Influencers:

Keep an eye on the work and insights of leading AI researchers, practitioners, and thought leaders. Following them on social media, reading their blogs, and attending their talks can provide valuable perspectives on the future of AI.

Participate in Conferences and Webinars:

Attend AI conferences, workshops, and webinars to learn about the latest research, tools, and applications. These events offer opportunities to network with experts and gain firsthand knowledge of emerging trends.

Subscribe to AI Newsletters and Journals:

Subscribe to reputable AI newsletters, journals, and magazines that curate and summarize important developments in the field. This can help you stay informed without having to sift through vast amounts of information.

Join Online Communities and Forums:

Engage with online communities and forums dedicated to AI, such as Reddit's r/Machine Learning or specialized LinkedIn groups. These platforms allow you to discuss trends, share experiences, and seek advice from peers.

Leverage AI Research Platforms:

Utilize platforms like arXiv and Google Scholar to access the latest AI research papers. Staying current with academic research can provide insights into cutting-edge techniques and theoretical advancements.

Experiment with New Tools and Technologies:

Actively experiment with new AI tools, libraries, and frameworks as they become available. Hands-on experience is one of the best ways to understand the capabilities and limitations of emerging technologies.

Collaborate with Academia and Research Institutions:

Collaborate with universities and research institutions working on AI projects. These partnerships can provide access to advanced research, talented students, and potential innovations.

Continuously Upskill Your Team:

Encourage and facilitate ongoing learning and development for your team. Providing access to training courses, workshops, and certification programs can help your team stay skilled in the latest AI technologies.

By staying updated with AI trends and innovations, businesses can make informed decisions, identify new opportunities, and remain competitive in the ever-changing landscape of artificial intelligence.

Revisiting Our Advice with Expanded Insights

In the introduction, we briefly discussed our approach, but with the added background information throughout this book, we find it beneficial to delve deeper into these discussions.

For Small Non-Microsoft-Based Businesses:

Our guidance primarily caters to businesses entrenched in Microsoft technologies—like Word, Excel, PowerPoint, Office,

> ### Competitive Advantage
>
> **83 percent of well-known companies believe AI will help them maintain or gain a competitive edge, and 72 percent of executives view AI as the most significant business advantage for the future Business**
>
> ### DIT, ISU Corp

Access, SharePoint, Project, Azure, Teams, and programming in C# or VB.NET. If your organization predominantly uses other technologies, it's sensible to align your AI strategies similarly. For instance, if Google Workspace is your mainstay, Google AI services might be the more suitable choice for AI implementation. Similarly, if AWS is a core component of your infrastructure, leveraging AWS AI Services could be advantageous.

While C# and VB.NET developers, including ourselves, can and do successfully integrate Google and AWS AI services into applications, the key is to assess whether this aligns optimally with your existing tech ecosystem.

For Small Businesses with Access to C# or VB.NET Developers:

If you have in-house C# or VB.NET developers or reliable external developers, our prototype resources are effectively free. Setting up and running our prototypes might take a few days of developer time.

For Small Businesses Experienced in Microsoft Excel or Access:

Individuals with experience in Microsoft Excel or Access development are well-positioned to transition into developing with Power Platform and CoPilot, making this a viable route for small businesses looking to explore AI capabilities.

For Small Businesses Without Developers:

For small enterprises lacking in-house development capabilities and preferring not to delve into learning these skills, opting for web-based AI applications might be the best approach. We provide a list of such applications in the resources of our website (www.AInDotNet.com).

For Medium and Large Businesses:

We believe that medium to large enterprises have the resources to develop custom applications and should continue using the programming and DevOps technologies currently in place. For instance, if your development is predominantly in Java, it may not be beneficial to switch to C# or VB.NET just for AI applications—unless you already have established infrastructure and expertise in these languages. In such cases, sticking with your existing development environment is likely the most efficient and cost-effective strategy.

Overall, while we advocate for certain approaches based on our expertise with Microsoft technologies and AI development, it's crucial to tailor these strategies to fit your specific business context and technological landscape. We're here to assist, not to insist that one size fits all.

Part 4:
Implementing AI in Your Business

"Building an AI application is like assembling a puzzle; every piece, from data to algorithms, must fit perfectly to reveal the big picture."

— Anonymous

Chapter 8:
Building an AI Innovation Team

In this chapter, we focus on the critical task of building a dedicated AI innovation team, an essential element for the successful adoption and application of artificial intelligence within your organization. More than just assembling a group of skilled individuals, forming an AI innovation team involves creating a synergistic unit that combines diverse skills, perspectives, and roles. This team will spearhead AI initiatives from their inception through to their successful implementation.

We will outline the key roles and expertise necessary to constitute a comprehensive AI innovation team, including programmers, database administrators, project managers, and domain experts. We will also discuss strategies to cultivate a culture of collaboration, innovation, and ongoing learning among team members.

Additionally, this chapter will offer guidance on developing a clear strategy and roadmap for AI integration, ensuring that your AI innovation team's efforts are in sync with the broader organizational goals and objectives. By the end of this chapter, you will gain a thorough understanding of how to effectively establish and manage an AI innovation team that can adeptly handle the complexities of AI projects and drive significant transformation within your business.

Roles and People the Big Cloud Stores Say You Need

The Big Cloud stores (Azure, AWS, Google) often suggest that implementing AI successfully within an organization requires assembling a new, expensive team of specialists. Here is a breakdown of the roles these providers typically recommend, along with our perspective on prioritizing and potentially simplifying these roles based on your business's experience with AI:

Data Scientists:

Role: Analyze and interpret complex data to inform decision-making using statistical techniques and machine learning models.

Expertise: Proficiency in languages like Python or R, knowledge of machine learning algorithms, and data manipulation and visualization tools.

Our Take: Consider delaying projects that require a data scientist until you gain more AI experience. Explore whether existing roles like database administrators or software developers could handle the data aspects of AI projects.

AI Engineers:

Role: Design and build AI models and systems, integrating AI capabilities into applications.

Expertise: Strong programming skills and familiarity with AI frameworks like TensorFlow or PyTorch.

Our Take: Postpone projects needing an AI engineer until you are more seasoned in AI. There are many AI applications achievable without this specialization. Each of our future books will be about one of these applications.

Machine Learning Engineers:

Role: Develop algorithms and predictive models to enable machine learning from data.

Expertise: Machine learning algorithms, data modeling, and software engineering principles.

Our Take: Delay projects that require a machine learning engineer until you're more adept in AI, focusing first on projects that don't require this level of expertise. We will show you over a dozen AI applications that do not need an ML engineer.

> **Diverse Skill Sets**
>
> **Assemble a team with a mix of skills, including management, project managers, SMEs, developers, database administrator. Diversity in expertise fosters creativity and comprehensive problem-solving.**

Data Engineers:

Role: Manage and optimize data pipelines and infrastructure to support AI and data science workflows.

Expertise: Data warehousing, ETL processes, and big data technologies like Microsoft SQL Server.

Our Take: If facing large, complex data needs, consider utilizing your existing database administrators.

Prompt Engineers:

Role: Develop and refine prompts for large language models (LLMs).

Expertise: Expertise in crafting effective LLM prompts.

Our Take: As you begin using LLMs, understanding prompt engineering becomes crucial. However, we advocate for widespread learning of prompt engineering, which will be covered in our upcoming publications. If you have one individual who is really into prompt engineering, definitely encourage them. They will be your prompt expert on the team, just as your database administrator is your data expert on the team.

Project Managers:

Role: Manage the AI project lifecycle to ensure timely delivery within budget and scope.

Expertise: Project management, AI project lifecycle knowledge, and team coordination.

Our Take: Relax traditional software project management during the prototyping. Essential once an AI application progresses beyond the prototype phase.

Domain Experts (Stakeholders or SMEs):

Role: Provide sector-specific insights to steer AI development toward addressing pertinent business challenges.

Expertise: In-depth industry knowledge and understanding of AI's potential impact.

Our Take: They are crucial for transitioning an AI application from prototype to MVP, as their insights and testing feedback are invaluable.

Innovation Culture

Foster an innovation-friendly culture where experimentation is encouraged and failures are seen as learning opportunities. Create a safe environment for team members to share and test new ideas.

Ethical, Legal Security Advisors:

Role: Ensure AI implementations adhere to ethical, legal, security requirements.

Expertise: AI ethics, data privacy laws, compliance regulations, security.

Our Take: While often overlooked, legal advisors are vital to navigate the complex regulatory landscape of AI. You should be able to use your regular people for this.

For large enterprises with substantial budgets, assembling a full team comprising these roles may be feasible. However, for most businesses, these roles can be streamlined or integrated into existing positions to reduce costs and focus on building practical, scalable, low-risk, low-cost AI solutions.

What People You Really Need

In this section, we'll identify the essential personnel you really need to drive successful AI integration in your organization, from management to developers.

Management/Executive Support:

Role: To foster innovation, it's critical to have the backing of top-level management, as productivity may initially dip. Executives must provide commitment and facilitate collaboration, particularly with teams that are hesitant about adopting new technologies.

Importance: Executive support is crucial for securing the resources needed and for persuading other departments to collaborate with the AI Innovation Team.

Project Manager:

Role: For projects beyond the prototype phase, such as those involving MVPs or transitioning MVPs to production-ready applications, the role of a project manager becomes essential.

Importance: We recommend that the project manager also oversees the AI Innovation Team to ensure coherent and focused project execution

Stakeholders/Subject Matter Experts (SMEs):

Role: Managers or directors of business processes who agree to pilot AI applications. They bring a deep understanding of operational needs and provide a real-world context for testing and refining AI solutions.

Importance: It's vital to engage proactive and innovation-minded SMEs who are open to experimenting and adopting new technologies. An SME resistant to change can significantly hinder the development and adoption of AI solutions.

Business Requirements Analyst:

Role: A business requirements analyst is crucial when applying AI to a business. They identify requirements, extract use cases, and translate communications between technical and business teams. Their tasks include feasibility analysis, scope definition, risk management, data analysis and validation, stakeholder management, identifying training needs, defining metrics and KPIs, and evaluating ROI. They provide independent analysis to determine which projects should be shelved and which offer the most value and should be prioritized.

Programmers (Developers):

Role: A robust team of developers, particularly those skilled in C# and/or VB.NET, is invaluable. Your first choice should be senior developers eager to explore new technologies, followed by those experienced in programming with Excel or Access. Developers proficient in other languages can add value.

Importance: For organizations lacking in-house capabilities, consider partnering with a software development firm. For smaller teams, a pairing of a dedicated SME and a developer can often suffice.

Database Administrators:

Role: Some AI applications have huge data requirements. .NET developers are used to working on applications with huge data

140

requirements and can handle probably 80 percent of data requirements.

Importance: Although database administrators are not required for simple data tasks, having them available for advice and to perform complex data tasks will help your innovation team.

Scaling Innovation According to Company Size:

Small Companies: Innovation must be cost-effective. Small companies should leverage their existing resources creatively to pilot AI initiatives without the burden of large budgets. People will have to take on multiple roles.

Medium-Sized Companies: These organizations may have more capital but still need to manage their innovation budgets carefully. Excessive spending on each prototype or maintaining full control over every AI application can be financially unsustainable. Start small. Grow iteratively as you see benefit.

Following Our Guides:

If you possess C# or VB.NET developers, our upcoming books will be an invaluable resource. We provide free C# prototype code, which VB.NET programmers can readily adapt. This approach is not only cost-effective and straightforward but also represents the lowest risk and most viable pathway for integrating AI into your operations.

By aligning the roles and expertise outlined above with the specific needs and scale of your company, you can set a solid foundation for the successful integration and utilization of AI technology.

Strategy for AI Implementation

1. Define Clear Objectives: Establish specific goals for AI implementation that align with the organization's overall strategy.

2. Assess Data Readiness: Evaluate the quality, availability, and accessibility of data required for AI projects. Some projects require very little data. Others require a lot of data, as well as extract, transform, load (ETL), and data cleansing. A data scientist or database administrator is your best bet for this job with a .NET programmer as a close second, given their familiarity with data-driven applications.

3. Develop a Roadmap: Create a phased plan that outlines the steps, timelines, and milestones for AI adoption. Early on, your roadmap will change dramatically. As your AI applications mature, your roadmap will become more stable.

4. Foster Collaboration: Encourage cross-functional collaboration between the AI team and other departments to ensure alignment and integration.

142

5. Invest in Training: Provide ongoing learning opportunities for the team to stay updated with the latest AI technologies and methodologies.

6. Monitor and Iterate: Regularly assess the performance of AI initiatives and make adjustments as needed to optimize outcomes.

By assembling a diverse team with the right roles and expertise and adopting a strategic approach to AI implementation, organizations can effectively leverage AI to drive innovation and achieve their business objectives.

Developing a roadmap for AI adoption

Creating a strategic roadmap is crucial for the successful adoption of AI within your organization. A well-defined roadmap provides a clear path forward, outlining the steps, milestones, and goals necessary for implementing AI solutions effectively. Here's how to develop a roadmap for AI adoption:

> **Clear Vision and Goals**
>
> **Define a clear vision and set achievable goals. Ensure every team member understands the mission and their role in achieving it.**

1. Define Your AI Vision and Objectives:

Start by establishing a clear vision for how AI will be used in your organization. Identify the specific objectives and outcomes you aim to achieve with AI, such as improving customer experience, enhancing operational efficiency, or driving innovation.

2. Assess Your Current Capabilities:

Conduct a thorough assessment of your organization's current technology infrastructure, data readiness, and team skills. This will help you identify gaps and areas that need improvement to support AI initiatives.

3. Prioritize Use Cases:

Based on the AI applications we covered in this book, your objectives and capabilities, identify and prioritize AI use cases that align with your business goals. Focus on areas where AI can provide significant value and impact.

4. Develop a Data Strategy:

Data is the foundation of AI. Develop a strategy for data collection, management, and governance to ensure that you have high-quality, relevant data to train and deploy AI models.

5. Build or Enhance Your AI Team:

Ensure that you have the right team in place to drive AI initiatives. This may involve hiring new talent, upskilling existing employees, or partnering with external AI experts.

6. Select AI Tools and Platforms:

Choose the appropriate AI tools and platforms that align with your use cases and technical requirements. Consider factors such as scalability, integration capabilities, and support for your chosen AI technologies.

7. Plan for Implementation and Integration:

Outline the steps for implementing AI solutions, including model development, testing, and integration into existing systems and processes. Address any technical and organizational challenges that may arise.

8. Establish Metrics and KPIs:

As AI applications start to mature (not at prototype stage), define key performance indicators (KPIs) and metrics to measure the success of your AI initiatives. Regularly track and evaluate progress against these metrics.

9. Create a Governance, Ethics, Security Framework:

Develop a framework for AI governance, ethics, and security to ensure responsible use of AI, including considerations for transparency, fairness, privacy, and security.

10. Iterate and Scale:

AI adoption is an ongoing process. Continuously iterate on your AI solutions based on feedback and results. Scale successful AI applications across the organization to maximize impact.

By following these steps, you can develop a comprehensive roadmap for AI adoption that guides your organization toward achieving its AI goals and realizing the full potential of artificial intelligence.

When you first start working on AI applications, expect your roadmap to change often. Over time, your roadmap will take on more structure.

Benefits of a Cash Reward System for Innovation

Do you want to put everyone in your company on the secondary innovation team and get everyone motivated to innovate?

Implementing a cash reward system for AI innovation ideas in a business can be a powerful motivator, but it requires careful planning and oversight. Here's an in-depth look at the potential benefits, challenges, and best practices for setting up such a system:

- Increased Motivation and Engagement: Cash rewards can significantly motivate employees to think creatively and contribute innovative ideas.

- Boost in Innovation: Offering a tangible incentive can encourage a higher volume of innovative ideas, potentially leading to breakthroughs that might not have emerged otherwise.

- Enhanced Company Culture: A reward system can foster a culture of innovation where employees feel valued and recognized for their contributions.

- ROI-Driven: By tying rewards to ROI, the company ensures that only ideas with tangible benefits are rewarded, aligning innovation with business goals.

- Retention and Satisfaction: Employees who feel their ideas are valued and rewarded are likely to have higher job satisfaction and lower turnover rates.

Challenges and Considerations

Criteria for Payout:

- Measurable ROI: Establish clear and measurable criteria for what constitutes a successful idea. For example, an idea should demonstrate a specific ROI, such as a 5x or 10x return.

- Verification Process: Implement a robust verification process to ensure that the claimed savings or ROI is accurate and attributable to the innovation.

- Percentage of Savings: Setting the payout as a percentage of the savings can be effective. For instance, if an idea saves $10,000 annually, a 10 percent payout ($1,000) could be a fair reward.

- The person must be an employee to submit ideas and must still be employed when the payout occurs (no temporary or non-employees).

Potential for Fraud:

- Collusion: Department heads and employees might collude to fabricate or exaggerate the benefits of an idea. To mitigate this, involve multiple stakeholders in the evaluation process and conduct periodic audits.

- Implementation Costs: Ensure that the cost of implementing the idea is accounted for when calculating ROI. An idea that saves money but costs a lot to implement might not be worth pursuing.

Sustainability:

- Long-term Impact: Consider the long-term impact of the ideas. Ensure that innovations provide sustainable benefits rather than short-term gains.

- Continuous Improvement: Encourage a culture of continuous improvement where employees are motivated to keep innovating rather than resting on their laurels after receiving a reward.

Pros and Cons of Cash Rewards for Innovation

Pros

- Direct Incentive: Cash is a straightforward and universally appreciated reward.

- Clear Value Proposition: Employees can see the direct benefit of their contributions.

- Scalable: The system can scale with the company's size and the number of innovative ideas generated.

Cons

- Risk of Quantity Over Quality: Employees might focus on generating numerous ideas rather than high-quality, impactful ones.

- Administrative Overhead: Managing the reward system, verifying ideas, and calculating ROI can add administrative burdens.

- Potential for Inequity: If not managed carefully, the system could lead to perceptions of favoritism or unfairness.

Best Practices for Implementation

1. Transparent Criteria: Clearly define the criteria for what constitutes an innovative idea and how the ROI will be calculated.

2. Multilevel Review: Implement a multilevel review process to evaluate ideas, including cross-departmental teams, to prevent collusion.

3. Regular Audits: Conduct regular audits of the reward system to ensure its integrity and fairness.

4. Feedback Loop: Create a feedback loop where employees can see the impact of their ideas and understand why some ideas are not selected.

5. Diverse Rewards: Consider offering a mix of cash rewards and other incentives, such as public recognition, additional time off, or professional development opportunities.

6. Have your AI Innovation Team vote on the best employee ideas to prototype.

7. Perhaps the manager of the department where the idea would be implemented has to abstain from judging the idea (if they are on the AI Innovation Team).

8. Warn employees that it can take more than one year from idea submission to selection, to prototype, to MVP, to evaluation of ROI.

What Traits Do You Want the People on Your Innovation Team to Have?

Curiosity: Innovative individuals have a strong desire to learn and understand new things. They ask questions, seek out new information, and are constantly exploring.

Creativity: They can think outside the box, generating original ideas and solutions. Creativity enables them to see possibilities that others might miss.

Problem-solving Skills: Innovators excel at identifying problems and devising effective solutions. They enjoy tackling challenges and can think critically.

Open-mindedness: They are open to new ideas and different perspectives. They are willing to challenge the status quo and embrace change.

Resilience: Innovation often involves failure before success. Resilient individuals can bounce back from setbacks and remain persistent in their efforts.

A cash reward system for AI innovation can drive significant benefits for a business if implemented thoughtfully. By ensuring transparent criteria, a robust verification process, and regular audits, businesses can mitigate potential downsides and foster a culture of sustained innovation and engagement among employees.

Collaboration: Innovation is often a team effort. Collaborative individuals work well with others, share ideas freely, and build on each other's contributions.

Passion: They are passionate about their work and driven by a genuine interest in the projects they undertake. This enthusiasm can inspire and motivate the entire team.

Adaptability: They can adjust quickly to new situations and pivot when necessary. Adaptability allows them to thrive in dynamic and unpredictable environments.

Analytical Thinking: They can break down complex problems into manageable parts and understand the underlying systems. Analytical thinkers are adept at finding patterns and connections.

Visionary Thinking: They can envision the future and understand how their ideas can be implemented to create long-term value.

Some people are more innovative than others due to a combination of innate traits, experiences, and environmental factors:

Innate Traits: Natural curiosity, creativity, and problem-solving abilities can be inherent traits that make some individuals more innovative.

Experiences: Diverse experiences and exposure to different fields, cultures, and ideas can foster innovative thinking.

Environment: Supportive environments that encourage risk-taking, experimentation, and learning from failure can nurture innovation. Access to resources, mentorship, and collaboration opportunities also play a significant role.

Mindset: A growth mindset, which embraces learning and improvement, contributes to a person's ability to innovate. Those with a fixed mindset may struggle to see beyond their current capabilities.

By seeking individuals with these qualities and fostering an environment that supports innovation, businesses can build highly effective innovation teams. Who does this describe in your business?

Chapter 9:
From Prototype to Production

Transitioning from an AI prototype to a production-ready solution is a critical step in the journey of AI adoption within an organization. In this chapter, we will explore the key considerations, challenges, and best practices for moving AI projects from the experimental stage to full-scale deployment.

We'll delve into the process of evaluating the feasibility and impact of AI prototypes, ensuring they meet business requirements and deliver tangible value. Additionally, we'll discuss strategies for scaling AI solutions, including infrastructure considerations, integration with existing systems, and managing data pipelines.

Moreover, this chapter will cover important aspects of production deployment, such as monitoring, maintenance, and continuous improvement of AI models. We'll also address the organizational and cultural shifts required to support the successful implementation of AI in a production environment.

By the end of this chapter, you'll have a comprehensive understanding of the steps and considerations involved in transforming AI prototypes into robust, scalable solutions that drive innovation and business growth.

Identifying Suitable Business Problems for AI Solutions

Identifying suitable business problems for AI solutions is crucial for successful implementation within an organization. Here are key steps to pinpoint problems that are well-suited for AI solutions:

Align with Business Goals:

Ensure that the problems you choose to address with AI are aligned with the overall strategic goals and objectives of your organization. This alignment guarantees that AI solutions contribute to meaningful outcomes.

Assess Data Availability:

Evaluate the availability and quality of data related to the problem. Some AI solutions rely heavily on data, so having access to relevant, clean, and sufficient data is crucial for building effective models.

Identify High-Impact Areas:

Focus on areas where AI can provide significant value, such as improving customer experience, enhancing operational efficiency, or generating new revenue streams. Prioritize problems that have a clear potential for impact.

Consider Feasibility:

Assess the technical feasibility of applying AI to the problem. This includes evaluating the complexity of the problem, the availability of AI tools and technologies, and the expertise required to develop and implement the solution.

Analyze ROI Potential:

Estimate the potential return on investment (ROI) for solving the problem with AI. Consider the costs involved in developing and deploying the solution, as well as the expected benefits and savings.

Evaluate Scalability:

Consider whether the AI solution can be scaled across the organization or applied to other similar problems. Scalability is important for maximizing the impact and value of AI investments.

Understand Regulatory, Ethical, Security Implications:

Be aware of any regulatory requirements or ethical considerations related to the problem and the proposed AI solution. Compliance and ethical use of AI are essential for responsible implementation.

Consult with Stakeholders:

Engage with key stakeholders, including business leaders, domain experts, and end-users to gather insights and validate the relevance and importance of the problem.

By following these steps, organizations can effectively identify business problems that are well-suited for AI solutions, ensuring that their AI initiatives are targeted, impactful, and aligned with their strategic objectives.

Testing, improving, and deploying AI applications

Testing AI Applications:

Unit Testing: Begin with unit tests to verify that individual components of the AI application operate correctly.

Integration Testing: Test the integration of different components to ensure seamless functionality.

Performance Testing: Evaluate the AI model's performance, including accuracy, speed, and resource consumption.

Validation Testing: Use a separate validation dataset to assess the model's generalization ability and prevent overfitting.

Security Testing: Conduct security tests to identify vulnerabilities and ensure that the application is protected against potential threats.

By using C# and VB.NET for AI applications, you should be able to use your regular testing methods. That is one of the huge advantages to using .NET.

Improving AI Applications:

Feedback Loop: Establish a feedback loop to continuously gather insights from the application's performance and user interactions. Always provide a way for users to flag inaccurate outputs. Do not require user feedback. Many operations will perform great. Make it easy for the user to offer constructive criticism, feedback, and suggestions.

Model Refinement: Use feedback to refine and retrain the AI model, addressing any identified shortcomings or biases.

Feature Engineering: For AI applications that have data features, experiment with different features and data preprocessing techniques to enhance the model's predictive power.

Hyperparameter Tuning: For AI applications that have hyperparameters, optimize the model's hyperparameters to improve performance and efficiency.

Source Control: Use source control systems to manage code changes and collaborate effectively with other developers. Another huge advantage of using existing .NET development resources.

Deploying AI Applications:

Deployment Strategy: Choose a deployment strategy that aligns with your application's requirements, whether cloud-based, on-premises, or edge deployment.

Monitoring and Maintenance: Implement monitoring tools to track the application's performance and health in real time. Set up a maintenance plan to address issues promptly.

Scalability: Ensure that the deployment infrastructure can scale to handle increased loads and data volumes as the application grows.

Security: Implement security measures to protect the application and its data, including encryption, access controls, and regular security audits.

By using C# and VB.NET for AI applications, you should be able to use your regular deployment methods.

User Training and Adoption:

User Training: Provide training and support to help users understand and effectively use the AI application.

- Change Management: Some people are afraid of innovation and change. Address any resistance to change and foster a culture of innovation and adaptation among stakeholders and their users.

Avoid Worshipping Shiny New Objects: Some users believe that new technology is always better and infallible. This is a misconception! We observed a similar phenomenon when computers and the Internet were first introduced. Use this analogy with users: just as you don't believe everything a computer or the Internet tells you, approach AI outputs with the same level of scrutiny.

Continuous Improvement:

Agile, Iterative Development: Treat deployment as the start of an ongoing process of improvement. Continuously update and enhance the AI application based on user feedback and evolving business needs.

By incorporating these elements, organizations can ensure that their AI applications are thoroughly tested, securely deployed, and continuously improved, leading to successful and sustainable AI implementation.

Expectations for Production Code

Production software is typically more robust, reliable, and user-friendly compared to prototypes. Here are some key functionalities and features expected in production software that might not be present in prototypes:

Create your AI functionality in a library (Visual Studio Project)

Creating libraries of functionality when writing computer code offers several advantages, including:

Code Reusability

Modularity: Libraries allow developers to create reusable pieces of code that can be used across multiple projects. This reduces redundancy and saves development time.

Consistency: By using a library, developers ensure consistent implementation of functionality across different applications.

Maintenance and Updates

Ease of Maintenance: Libraries encapsulate functionality in a single place, making it easier to maintain and update. When a bug is fixed or an improvement is made in the library, all projects using that library benefit from the update.

Version Control: Libraries can be versioned, allowing developers to manage and track changes over time. This helps in maintaining compatibility with different versions of the library.

Efficiency and Performance

Optimization: Libraries can be optimized for performance, ensuring that common functionalities run efficiently. This can lead to overall performance improvements in applications using the library.

Resource Management: Libraries can include efficient algorithms and data structures, which can help manage resources better, such as memory and processing power.

Collaboration and Standardization

Team Collaboration: Libraries promote collaboration among developers by providing a shared codebase. This encourages best practices and coding standards within a team.

Company Contributions: Libraries benefit from company contributions, leading to faster identification of bugs, new features, and overall improvement in quality.

Abstraction and Simplification

Simplified Interfaces: Libraries often provide high-level interfaces that simplify complex operations. This abstraction makes it easier for developers to use advanced functionalities without needing to understand the underlying implementation details.

Focus on Business Logic: By leveraging libraries, developers can focus more on the unique aspects of their applications rather than on implementing common functionalities from scratch.

Scalability and Extensibility

Scalability: Libraries can be designed to scale with the application, providing robust solutions that handle increased load or complexity.

Extensibility: Libraries can be extended with additional functionalities as needed, allowing developers to build upon existing code without reinventing the wheel.

Testing and Reliability

Pre-Tested Code: Libraries often come with extensive testing, reducing the likelihood of bugs in their functionality. This increases the reliability of applications that use these libraries.

Unit Testing: Libraries can be tested independently from the main application, ensuring that they work correctly before being integrated.

By creating and utilizing libraries, developers can enhance productivity, improve code quality, and facilitate better project management, ultimately leading to more robust and maintainable software solutions.

To apply the library, you look at the requirements and put a simple interface on the front of the library. For example, you can quickly and easily create Web API, Console Application, Web User Interface, Desktop User Interface, call the library directly from an application, etc.

Logging

Logging in software programming offers numerous advantages that enhance the development process, maintenance, and overall reliability of software systems. Here are some key benefits:

Debugging and Troubleshooting

Error Diagnosis: Logs provide detailed information about the state of the application at various points in time, helping developers identify and diagnose errors or bugs.

Contextual Information: Logs can capture the context around errors, such as input parameters and system states, making it easier to understand what went wrong.

Monitoring and Maintenance

Performance Monitoring: Logs can track performance metrics, such as response times and resource utilization, allowing developers to identify and address performance bottlenecks.

System Health: Regular logging of system health indicators can help in proactive maintenance, identifying potential issues before they become critical.

Security and Compliance

Audit Trails: Logs provide an audit trail of system activities, which is essential for security audits and regulatory compliance. This includes tracking user actions, data access, and system changes.

Intrusion Detection: Security logs can help in detecting unauthorized access or suspicious activities, aiding in the prevention of security breaches.

User Behavior Analysis

Usage Patterns: Logs can capture user interactions with the system, providing insights into usage patterns and user behavior.

Feature Usage: By analyzing logs, developers can determine which features are most used and which are underutilized, guiding future development priorities.

Accountability and Traceability

Change Tracking: Logs can record changes made to the system, such as configuration changes or code updates, making it easier to trace issues back to specific changes.

Responsibility: Logs can help attribute actions to specific users or processes, enhancing accountability within the development and operations teams.

Incident Response

Root Cause Analysis: Detailed logs enable thorough root cause analysis during incident response, helping teams to understand the sequence of events leading up to an issue.

Post-Mortem Analysis: Logs provide a comprehensive record that can be reviewed during post-mortem analysis to learn from incidents and prevent future occurrences.

Continuous Improvement

Feedback Loop: Logs serve as a feedback loop, providing real-time information about the system's behavior and performance, which can be used to make iterative improvements.

Benchmarking: Historical log data can be used to benchmark system performance and measure the impact of changes or optimizations over time.

Communication and Collaboration

Shared Information: Logs can be shared across development, operations, and support teams, facilitating better communication and collaboration when addressing issues.

Documentation: Logs serve as a form of documentation, capturing the operational history of the system and providing valuable insights for new team members.

Automation and Alerting

Automated Alerts: Logs can be integrated with monitoring tools to trigger automated alerts based on predefined conditions, enabling rapid response to critical issues.

Automated Analysis: Advanced logging frameworks can analyze log data in real-time, providing automated insights and recommendations.

Compliance, Legal, Security Protection

Regulatory Compliance: Many industries require logging to ensure compliance with regulations and standards and that organizations meet legal requirements.

Legal Evidence: Logs can serve as legal evidence in disputes, providing a reliable record of system activities and user actions.

In summary, logging is a vital practice in software development and operations, offering numerous benefits that contribute to the stability, security, and continuous improvement of software systems. By implementing comprehensive logging strategies, organizations can enhance their ability to monitor, diagnose, and optimize their applications effectively.

Exception and Error Handling

Error handling, and writing the error to the log file, shows that you as a programmer were smart enough to anticipate this error and to be able to handle it.

Exception handling is a catch all for errors that you did not anticipate.

We typically incorporate System.Reflection, as in MethodBase.GetCurrentMethod(), for each entry in the log file. This tells you the date, time, Assembly (DLL), version, Class, and function that wrote the log entry.

For exceptions, we add the exception Message and the stack trace.

For example, we get a message that an exception occurred. When we go to log file and search for exception, it gives us the assembly (DLL), version, class, and line number.

We go into version control, find that version of the DLL, find the class, and go to the line number to see exactly what line in the code caused the exception. Based on that information, we can quickly and easily determine how to fix the problem.

By catching specific exceptions first and general exceptions last, you get the benefits of specific detailed exception messages and the coverage of all exceptions.

Application Monitoring

You need a mechanism to notify you when something is not working correctly. There are many ways to do this. Some prefer to just send an email when an error or exception occurs. Others prefer to have a remote monitoring system where your application periodically sends a signal to signal it's running and sends exceptions to notify you. It's great if the notification tells you the server name (or IP address), location of log files on the server, server log file name, and date and time of error or exception. And the error or exception that occurred.

Security Measures

Authentication and Authorization: Production systems implement strong authentication and authorization processes to secure user access.

Data Encryption: Data at rest and in transit is often encrypted to protect sensitive information.

Security Auditing: Logs and monitoring for security-related events to detect and respond to potential breaches.

Performance Optimization

Optimized Code: Production code is optimized for performance, including efficient algorithms and resource management.

Caching and Load Balancing: Techniques like caching and load balancing are used to enhance performance and scalability.

Scalability

Horizontal and Vertical Scaling: Production software is designed to scale both horizontally (adding more machines) and vertically (adding more power to existing machines).

Elasticity: The ability to automatically adjust resources based on demand.

Reliability and Availability

Redundancy: Implementing redundancy for critical components to ensure high availability.

Failover Mechanisms: Systems are designed with failover mechanisms to maintain service during failures.

User Interface and Experience

User-Friendly Design: A polished and intuitive user interface designed for ease of use.

Accessibility: Compliance with accessibility standards to ensure the software is usable by people with disabilities.

Documentation and Support

User Documentation: Comprehensive user manuals, help files, and online documentation.

Support Infrastructure: Support infrastructure, including FAQs, customer service, and technical support.

Testing and Quality Assurance

Automated Testing: Extensive automated testing, including unit tests, integration tests, and end-to-end tests.

Load Testing: Load testing to ensure the software performs well under expected and peak loads.

Data Management

Backup and Recovery: Regular data backup processes and recovery plans.

Data Integrity: Mechanisms to ensure data consistency and integrity.

Compliance and Regulatory

Regulatory Compliance: Adherence to industry regulations and standards.

Audit Trails: Maintaining detailed audit trails for compliance and security purposes.

Internationalization and Localization

Multilingual Support: Support for multiple languages and regional settings.

Localization: Adaptation of content and interfaces for different cultures and regions.

Integration and Interoperability

API Integration: Well-defined APIs for integration with other systems and services.

Interoperability: Ensuring the software can work seamlessly with other applications and platforms.

Deployment and Maintenance

Automated Deployment: Tools and processes for automated deployment and continuous integration/continuous deployment (CI/CD).

Maintenance Tools: Tools for routine maintenance, updates, and patches.

Feedback Mechanisms

User Feedback: Built-in mechanisms to collect user feedback and usage analytics.

Error Reporting: Automated error reporting to capture and report issues.

Compliance with Privacy and Ethical Standards

Privacy Policies: Implementation of privacy policies to protect user data.

Ethical Considerations: Addressing ethical considerations in software design and implementation.

In summary, production software encompasses a range of functionalities that ensure it is secure, reliable, efficient, and user-friendly, meeting the needs of end-users and stakeholders in real-world environments. Prototypes, on the other hand, focus on demonstrating core functionality and concepts, often lacking these comprehensive features.

Production software has a lot of important details that prototypes and minimally viable products may not. The good news is, if your company has been developing .NET applications, you should already have most of these details in use and add the same or similar functionality to AI applications.

Chapter 10:
Answers to Your AI Concerns

How does your plan for Applying AI to Business work?

Our Applying AI to Business Blueprint is a structured approach to integrating artificial intelligence into your organization. Here's how it works:

1. Set up Your AI Innovation Team:

   a) Put out a call for coworkers interested in joining the AI Innovation Team.

   b) Look for individuals who enjoy innovation and challenges and are not afraid to fail. People that are great problem solvers and can work on complex problems independently.

   c) Obtain support from upper management to endorse the group's goals, overcome roadblocks, and provide guidance.

   d) Appoint at least one project manager to oversee the team and projects.

   e) Include at least one stakeholder or subject matter expert (SME) to provide insights on requirements and use cases and to test prototypes and products.

   f) Have at least one developer on the team or consider outside contractors for development services.

   g) Schedule regular bi-weekly meetings to keep the team aligned and progressing.

2. Start with Our First Book:

a) Purchase a copy of this first book for each team member. This ensures everyone starts from the same point and understands the road map ahead.

b) Form a book club where everyone reads and discusses the concepts and considers how to implement AI in your business.

c) Once the team has studied the first book, acquire a copy of our first book on core AI applications for each member. These books focus on a specific AI tool, application, or service and provides free C# prototype code, which can be converted to VB.NET.

d) Have your developer get the code running before the next AI Innovation Team meeting. If the AI application is a website or web API, share the URL with the team.

e) Encourage the team to interact with the prototype, noting what they like, dislike, and any missing features. Explore potential use cases for the AI tool in your business.

3. Repeat for Each Subsequent Book:

a) We plan to publish about 12 books on core AI applications.

b) Your AI Innovation Team will need to decide when to transition from studying one application to developing it or moving on to the next.

c) Having more than one developer can expedite progress. You can work on multiple AI prototypes concurrently.

d) Aim to advance the promising AI prototypes to a minimal viable product (MVP) or early production system quickly, where a regular software development team can take over development and maintenance.

e) Once an AI application is handed off to the regular software team, your AI Innovation Team developers can start on a new AI application prototype.

What Problems Do We Solve?

1. Other approaches require hiring new, expensive personnel with specialized skills. Our approach utilizes existing employees, leveraging their knowledge and expertise.

2. Other approaches necessitate investing in new, costly technologies, programming languages, services, systems, DevOps, and source control. Our approach utilizes predominantly existing technologies, programming languages, services, systems, and DevOps.

3. Other approaches, as estimated by Gartner, have an 80 percent failure rate. Our approach provides businesses with the source code for prototypes, increasing their chances of success.

4. Other approaches can cost up to $500,000 for a prototype. Our approach provides the prototype code to businesses for free.

5. Other approaches have a steep learning curve, requiring users to learn entirely new systems and processes. Our approach minimizes this curve by keeping most aspects familiar and covering essential concepts in one book.

6. Other approaches have long lead times from concept to prototype. Our approach accelerates this process. After reading the book and downloading the code, businesses can compile the prototype code and have a working prototype.

7. Other approaches, especially those involving external consultants, may raise concerns about the reuse of customer's code and the protection of proprietary information. Our approach, your business owns the source

code, ensuring that your proprietary secrets and advantage remain confidential and under your control.

For more information:

https://AInDotNet.com

KeithBaldwin@AInDotNet.com

Frequently Asked Questions

Why do you specify Microsoft-based businesses?

We specialize in Microsoft technologies because they are well-suited for most business applications. While AWS and Google offer great AI services, using Microsoft products within the Microsoft platform tends to be more straightforward.

Do your books work with VB.NET instead of C#?

Yes, our books work equally well for VB.NET. It's straightforward to convert C# code to VB.NET.

Would your books work for non-Microsoft businesses?

Yes, but there are differences between platforms. If you use Visual Studio but not C#, you can easily convert the code. If your applications use a compiled typed object-oriented programming language, continue using that environment.

Are you related to Microsoft, AWS, or Google?

No, we are independent of Microsoft, AWS, and Google. We have used their technologies for decades and believe they are great for business, but we do not represent these companies.

What are the advantages of incorporating AI into our business operations?

AI streamlines operations, automates routine tasks, and enhances decision-making through data-driven insights. It also opens doors to innovation, new products, and market penetration, providing a distinct competitive advantage and contributing to risk management.

How do we initiate AI integration and what prerequisites should we consider?

Form an AI Innovation Team from diverse departments to identify critical areas for AI. Begin with developing small-scale prototypes to experiment and gauge potential impact. We provide resources, including code and tutorials, to help your programmers implement AI solutions swiftly.

Can you provide examples of successful AI implementations relevant to our industry?

This book includes a collection of hundreds of AI use cases across various sectors, illustrating AI's capabilities in enhancing efficiency, innovation, and decision-making. These examples can inspire AI strategies tailored to your business.

How can we effectively integrate AI with our existing Microsoft technologies?

Microsoft tools like Azure Machine Learning and Cognitive Services are designed to work seamlessly with existing systems. We provide comprehensive guidance on utilizing these technologies to enhance your business operations.

What are the costs involved in developing and maintaining AI prototypes?

We emphasize low-cost, quick-to-develop, and low-risk solutions using existing Microsoft technologies. This approach facilitates cost-effective exploration of AI capabilities without heavy initial investment.

How can we maintain data security and privacy when implementing AI in our systems?

Our approach adheres to the same security practices as your existing applications. This ensures that protective measures for securing sensitive information and complying with data protection laws are extended to AI implementations.

What kind of support and training do you offer for AI adoption?

Our company offers comprehensive support and training for AI adoption to ensure your business can effectively implement and leverage AI technologies. We have the capability to develop AI solutions at various stages, from prototypes and minimally viable products to production-ready products. With decades of experience developing applications based on Microsoft technologies, our team is well-equipped to guide you through the AI integration process.

Our services are tailored to meet your specific needs. Whether you are looking to develop standalone AI applications or services or integrate AI into your existing applications, we have the expertise to make it happen. Our support extends beyond development, offering ongoing training and consulting services to ensure that your team is equipped to manage and optimize your AI solutions. By partnering with us, you gain access to a wealth of knowledge and experience in both AI and Microsoft technologies, ensuring a smooth and successful adoption of AI in your business.

How can AI be tailored to meet our specific business requirements?

AI can be integrated into existing applications like any other tool or service. Our strategy focuses on selecting AI tools that align with your business objectives and seamlessly integrating them into your infrastructure.

What is the expected timeline for developing and deploying an AI prototype?

With our resources, developing and deploying an AI prototype can take a few days. Your team can experiment with the prototype, perform evaluations, and gather feedback in a practical timeframe.

How do we evaluate the success of our AI initiatives?

Engage stakeholders and subject matter experts (SMEs) early to define success metrics. Regular feedback and flexible deployment strategies ensure that AI solutions are well-received and maximally beneficial.

Common Concerns and Fears

How can we ensure that implementing AI does not become overly complex or require more technical expertise than we currently possess?

Our strategic approach minimizes complexity, cost, and risk by integrating AI solutions with minimal disruption to your existing systems. We educate your team to manage AI initiatives effectively over the long term.

How can we ensure that the initial investment and ongoing costs of developing and maintaining AI solutions are manageable and fit within our budget?

We provide complete source code, use widely available Microsoft technologies, and emphasize team education to minimize costs and build internal expertise.

How can we ensure that integrating AI into our existing systems and workflows will be seamless and minimally disruptive?

We align our development processes with your established practices, use incremental updates, and provide comprehensive training to ensure smooth integration.

How can we protect our sensitive information from breaches and misuse when implementing AI solutions?

We adhere to rigorous security standards, deploy AI services in secure environments, and maintain consistency in our integration processes.

How can we ensure that our team is equipped with the necessary skills and knowledge to effectively leverage AI in our business?

Our books provide essential knowledge for creating working prototypes and serve as a launchpad for specialized AI study, enabling your team to gain practical experience.

How can we ensure that our investment in AI will yield tangible benefits and enhance our bottom line?

Adopting an iterative approach to innovation minimizes risks and maximizes resource allocation to promising solutions, ensuring positive ROI.

How can we implement AI in a way that minimizes job losses and positively impacts our workforce?

AI can augment employees' capabilities, automating routine tasks and allowing workers to focus on more complex activities, fostering a more efficient and adaptable workforce.

How can we ensure that our use of AI complies with the legal and regulatory requirements specific to our industry?

We advise businesses to consult legal advisors to navigate AI regulations and ensure compliance with data protection laws and industry standards.

How can we ensure that our reliance on external vendors for AI solutions does not lead to being locked into proprietary systems or encountering issues with support and updates?

We provide source code and use standard development tools to minimize vendor lock-in, ensuring you maintain control over your AI solutions.

What distinguishes your AI approach from others and why should we choose you for our AI journey?

Our approach delivers practical, low-risk, and cost-effective AI solutions that integrate seamlessly with your existing infrastructure. We provide source code ownership and minimize disruption, offering user-friendly AI solutions without the high costs and hassles of traditional AI consultants.

How do you address fears that AI projects may not meet expectations, leading to wasted resources and unfulfilled objectives?

We define clear, measurable objectives, adopt an incremental approach, and involve stakeholders regularly to ensure AI projects align with business needs and deliver the intended value.

What are the potential risks of implementing AI in our business and how do you plan to mitigate them?

We prioritize data security, adopt phased integration, and implement transparent AI systems to mitigate risks and ensure successful AI integration.

Embracing AI for Future Success

As we approach the conclusion of our exploration into the transformative potential of artificial intelligence in business, it is important to reflect on the journey we have undertaken together. Throughout this book, we've delved into the complexities, challenges, and immense possibilities presented by AI. From understanding the basic principles of AI to seeing it in action across various industries and from building your first AI prototype to scaling up to full production, this journey has been designed to equip you with the knowledge and tools necessary for success in the AI-driven business landscape.

In this final section, we will revisit the key insights that can help fortify your strategy as you move forward. We will summarize the crucial lessons learned, reinforce the calls to action, and discuss ongoing learning opportunities that will help you stay ahead in a rapidly evolving field. Additionally, we will outline the support structures we have in place to assist you as you implement what you have learned.

Our goal is not just to inform but to inspire and empower you to take the steps that can transform your business operations and lead you to new heights of innovation and efficiency. Let's take a moment to encapsulate the valuable strategies and foresights shared, ensuring that you are well-prepared to navigate the future of AI in business.

Recap of Key Points

As we conclude this comprehensive guide, it's important to highlight the pivotal insights and core themes that have shaped our understanding of artificial intelligence and its application in the business environment. This recap serves not only as a summary but as a foundation upon which you can build and expand your AI initiatives.

1. Understanding AI: We began our journey with a thorough exploration of what AI is, its history, and its impact on society. The distinctions between AI, machine learning, deep learning, and generative AI were clarified to provide a solid conceptual framework.

2. AI in Business: We discussed why AI is indispensable for modern businesses, emphasizing how it solves complex problems, enhances efficiency, and drives innovation. Through various industry examples, we demonstrated AI's versatility and its role in streamlining operations and decision-making processes.

3. Building AI Applications: The steps to develop an AI prototype were outlined in detail. This included discussions on the necessary development resources, the integration of Microsoft and other technologies, and the iterative approach to refining AI solutions.

4. Implementing AI: Key strategies for forming an AI innovation team, transitioning from prototype to production, and the critical roles necessary for sustainable AI deployment were examined. This section provided a roadmap for embedding AI deeply and effectively within your organizational structure.

5. Ethical and Responsible AI: Throughout the book, we stressed the importance of ethical considerations. Ensuring that AI implementations are fair, transparent, and respectful of privacy remains a paramount concern as these technologies become more deeply integrated into our daily business practices.

6. Practical Guidance: Each chapter was designed not only to inform but also to equip you with practical tools and step-by-step instructions to engage actively with AI technologies. From leveraging existing Infrastructures like Microsoft platforms to navigating new tools like AutoML and TorchSharp, we provided actionable advice tailored to your needs.

By revisiting these key points, we reinforce the comprehensive nature of AI's role in business and ensure that you are well-prepared to tackle the challenges and opportunities it presents. As you move forward, keep these insights in mind as they will serve as guideposts on your ongoing journey with AI.

Lessons Learned

Throughout this book, we've journeyed through the multifaceted landscape of artificial intelligence, uncovering its capabilities and limitations and learning how best to harness its power in the business context. Here are some of the pivotal lessons learned that can help shape your approach to AI integration:

1. Start Small and Scale: One of the most critical lessons is the value of starting with small, manageable AI projects. This approach allows you to gauge the effectiveness of AI

177

solutions without overwhelming your resources and provides a practical learning curve for your team.

2. Interdisciplinary Collaboration is Key: AI is not just a technological upgrade but a transformative tool that impacts multiple aspects of business operations. Successful AI implementation often requires collaborative efforts across various departments—combining insights from IT, data science, business strategy, and even ethics.

3. Continuous Learning and Adaptation: AI technology is rapidly evolving. Staying informed and adaptable is crucial. This involves not only keeping up with new AI developments and technologies but also continually reassessing and refining your AI strategies to align with current business needs and technological capabilities.

4. Ethics Cannot Be an Afterthought: Ensuring that AI systems are ethical and transparent has emerged as a foundational requirement, not just a nice-to-have. This includes addressing biases in AI models, ensuring data privacy, and maintaining clear accountability for AI-driven decisions.

5. Integration Over Isolation: AI should not be siloed as a standalone tool but integrated seamlessly with existing systems and workflows. This integration helps in leveraging AI's full potential without disrupting the existing operational framework.

6. Empower Your Team: Equipping your team with the necessary skills and knowledge to work with AI is just as important as the technology itself. Investments in training and development not only prepare your workforce for AI but also enhance their ability to innovate and adapt.

7. Practicality Over Perfection: It's vital to focus on practical and actionable AI solutions that directly address specific business challenges. While it's easy to be drawn to the

allure of cutting-edge AI, the real value comes from its application to solve real-world problems.

8. Measure and Iterate: Establish clear metrics to measure the success of your AI initiatives. Use these metrics not only to gauge effectiveness but also as a feedback mechanism to iterate and improve your AI solutions.

These lessons form the bedrock of a strategic approach to AI in business. They underscore the necessity of a thoughtful, informed, and proactive strategy that aligns with both the technological landscape and your unique business goals. As you continue your journey with AI, keep these lessons at the forefront of your strategy to ensure that your AI initiatives are successful and sustainable.

High Level Call to Action

As we wrap up our exploration of artificial intelligence in the business context, it's important to transition from learning and understanding to action and implementation. Here are specific steps and initiatives you can undertake to begin or enhance your journey with AI:

1. Evaluate Your Current Technology Stack: Assess the current technologies and systems in use at your company. Identify potential integration points for AI technologies and consider where AI can create the most impact.

2. Identify Business Challenges: Pinpoint specific business challenges that could benefit from AI solutions. Start with problems where solutions can be quantified and measured, such as automating routine tasks, enhancing customer service, or improving decision-making processes.

3. Start a Pilot Project: Select a small, low-risk project to start your AI journey. Use this pilot project as a testbed to understand the nuances of AI integration, gather data, and measure outcomes. This approach allows for practical learning and minimal disruption.

4. Invest in Training: Ensure your team is prepared to work with new AI tools by investing in training and development. Our series of books will provide you with most of the training you need as well as free source code.

5. Leverage Expertise: Consider partnering with AI experts or consultants who can provide guidance and insights specific to your industry. Their experience can help accelerate your AI projects and avoid common pitfalls.

6. Scale With Confidence: Once your pilot project shows positive results, plan for a gradual rollout. Scale your AI implementations systematically to other parts of the business, ensuring that each step is manageable and results are monitored.

7. Stay Informed: Keep abreast of the latest AI advancements and trends. Join industry forums, subscribe to newsletters, and participate in discussions to stay updated.

8. Evaluate and Iterate: Continuously evaluate the performance of your AI solutions against the set objectives. Be prepared to iterate and make adjustments as necessary to align with evolving business needs and technological advancements.

9. Ethical Considerations: As you implement AI, continuously assess the ethical implications of your AI systems. Ensure that they are transparent, fair, and compliant with regulations.

Share Your Success: Once you achieve success with AI, share your experiences and learnings within and outside your organization. This not only positions your company as an innovator but also encourages a culture of learning and adaptation.

By following these steps, you are not just adopting technology; you are setting the stage for transformational change that can significantly enhance how your business operates. Let's take the insights and strategies from this book and turn them into actionable, impactful AI initiatives that drive real value for your business.

Continued Learning and Adaptation

The landscape of artificial intelligence is dynamic and ever-evolving, making continuous learning and adaptation fundamental for businesses aiming to leverage AI effectively. As we move forward, it is vital to embrace a culture of ongoing education and flexibility in adapting to new developments. Here are key strategies to ensure that your organization remains at the forefront of AI technology and practices:

1. Commit to Ongoing Education: Encourage your team to engage in continuous learning about AI. This can be facilitated through online courses, workshops, webinars, and conferences. Prioritize education not just for your tech teams but also for your management and operational staff to broaden the understanding of AI's capabilities and challenges across your organization.

2. Stay Connected with the AI Community: Engage with the broader AI community to exchange ideas and insights. This can include participating in forums, attending AI and tech meetups, and contributing to open-source AI projects. Networking with AI professionals can provide you with fresh perspectives and innovative ideas.

3. Follow Industry Trends: Keep up to date with the latest trends and developments in AI by subscribing to relevant publications, following thought leaders on social media, and monitoring significant breakthroughs in AI research. This will help you anticipate and react to changes in technology that could impact your business.

4. Experiment and Innovate: Foster a culture that encourages experimentation and innovation within your organization. Allow your team the freedom to try new approaches and technologies in a controlled environment. This can lead to

discoveries of how AI can solve problems in ways not previously considered.

5. Review and Refine AI Strategies Regularly: Set regular intervals to review your AI strategies and projects. This review should assess the effectiveness of current AI implementations and identify areas for improvement or potential scaling. Adjustments should be made based on performance data, feedback from users, and evolving business goals.

6. Adapt to Regulatory Changes: AI is a rapidly changing field not only in terms of technology but also in regulation. Stay informed about new regulations and ethical standards concerning AI and be prepared to adapt your practices to comply with these changes.

7. Leverage AI for Learning: Utilize AI tools themselves to aid in learning and adaptation. AI can help analyze the effectiveness of your business strategies, provide insights into market trends, and personalize learning paths for employees based on their progress and interests.

8. Cultivate Resilience: Prepare your organization to be resilient in the face of technological change. This means not only being reactive to changes but also proactive in implementing practices that can withstand shifts in the AI landscape.

By embedding these practices into your organization's DNA, you ensure that your business not only keeps pace with AI developments but also harnesses them to foster continuous growth and innovation.

Our Roadmap

We are a bootstrap startup passionate about applying AI to business using C# and VB.NET. We believe that leveraging AI with .NET languages is an overlooked sweet spot for achieving high functionality with minimal changes, low cost, and low risk. All that .NET development teams need is a bit of instruction and direction.

Please be patient as we start up. Things often take longer than expected, and priorities can shift based on feedback from our customers and audience. Developing new operations and systems takes time.

Our goal is to release one new book every one to two quarters (every three to six months). Although books are just a small part of our social media outreach, which in turn is a small part of our business, social media remains our primary marketing tool and is therefore important. Plus, we want to help businesses like yours— for the price of a book.

Future Books (AI Topics and Prototypes)

For future books, we want you to learn, try, and experiment with "quick wins." We've identified AI tools that are quick to learn, implement, and experiment with, providing the highest return on investment (ROI). Each book will have free prototype C# or VB.NET code. Here's our initial roadmap for future books:

1. This Introductory Book
2. AI Virtual Assistants
3. Chatbots
4. Anomaly Detection
5. Sentiment Analysis
6. Forecasting and Prediction (Regression)
7. Retrieval Augmented Generation (RAG)
8. Intelligent Document Processing (IDP)
9. Call Centers
10. Data Preparation and Synthetic Data
11. Computer Vision

12. Recommendation Systems

13. Operations Research and Optimization

14. Agents and Planning

15. Robotic Process Automation (RPA)

Each of these books will serve as another tool in your toolbox. We will provide you with instruction on the AI tool and free prototype C# or VB.NET code so that you can have the AI tool up and running in hours. Our aim is for readers to learn and explore quickly and easily with low cost and low risk.

Managing AI Projects

Starting a new book (and AI prototype) every quarter is ambitious and may be overwhelming for businesses to implement. Assuming everything operates optimally, the business has unlimited resources on their AI Innovation Team and their business only generates one minimally viable product (MVP) and one production system from each of our books, activities will look like:

Year	Quarter 1	Quarter 2	Quarter 4	Quarter 4
1	Setup AI Team	1 Prototype	2 Prototype	2 Prototype 1 MVP
2	2 Prototype 2 MVP	2 Prototype 2 MVP 1 Production	2 Prototype 2 MVP 2 Production	2 Prototype 2 MVP 3 Production
3	2 Prototype 2 MVP 4 Production	2 Prototype 2 MVP 5 Production	2 Prototype 2 MVP 6 Production	2 Prototype 2 MVP 7 Production

This table assumes your team starts one new book (AI tool and prototype) each quarter, it takes six months to go from prototype to MVP and 12 months to go from prototype to production system. These time estimates will vary widely depending on how fast your requirements can be defined, how many other AI projects you are working on simultaneously, other workloads, available resources, type of project, etc.

We stopped projections after year three because, by the third year, you are going to have so many AI tools and projects going into so many different departments and applications we don't think our linear prediction approach will accurately project your work load.

Assuming our roadmap holds, at the end of three years, you've developed 11 new prototypes (AI tools), nine new minimally viable products (MVPs), and put seven AI tools into production. And you've got four more of our books (and prototypes) to start.

Reality

Our previous assumption was that from each AI prototype, only one MVP and one production system will be developed. The reality is that each AI prototype could spawn multiple MVPs, and each MVP could spawn multiple production systems. We think that by year two or three, you will be resource constrained, your AI Innovation Team could be full time trying to learn, keep up with, evaluate the ROI of all of the AI projects that are going on.

We think that a more reasonable approach will be to start one new book (AI tool and prototype) every six months. Or maybe one new book each quarter for the first year and then switch to one new book every six months.

Note: This roadmap is subject to change. As we progress, we will adapt our plans based on new developments, technological advances, and your feedback. Our priority is to deliver valuable, relevant content that meets your needs and helps you succeed in applying AI to your business operations.

Specific Action Items for Implementing AI Innovation

Each business is different, so modify these action items for your business.

1. Start Your AI Innovation Team

   a) Define the Mission: Clearly articulate the team's mission, objectives, and expected outcomes to ensure alignment and focus.

2. Appoint a Leader

   a) Daily and Weekly Management: Select a capable project manager with an interest in innovation or someone with strong project management skills to lead the team's activities.

3. Announce the Formation of the AI Innovation Team

   a) Internal Communication: Use company-wide channels to announce the team's creation.

   b) Highlight Benefits: Emphasize the opportunities and benefits for participants.

   c) Select Members: Conduct interviews or assessments to ensure the right fit for the team.

4. Recruit Ideal Candidates

   a) Identify Skills and Attributes: Actively seek individuals with the innovative skills and attributes outlined in this book.

5. Equip Your Team with Knowledge

   a) Distribute the Book: Provide a copy of this book to each team member to ensure a shared knowledge base.

   b) Unified Understanding: Ensure everyone starts with the same understanding and direction.

6. Initiate a Book Club

   a) Regular Meetings: Schedule regular discussions, focusing on one or two chapters every week or two.

b) Encourage Engagement: Promote sharing of insights and real-world applications among team members.

7. Understand the Strategic Advantages

   a) Discuss Benefits: Review the strategic benefits of the outlined approach.

   b) Evaluate Alternatives: Discuss the limitations of low-code/no-code solutions and the high costs of big cloud providers versus the flexibility of custom .NET applications.

8. Review AI Use Cases

   a) Explore Use Cases: Examine the hundreds of AI use cases listed in the book.

   b) Download Resources: Access the Excel spreadsheet for AI use cases from our website.

   c) Analyze and Prioritize: Have team members analyze relevant use cases and rank them by potential value and ROI.

9. Understand the Development Process

   a) Stages of Development: Break down the stages from prototype to minimally viable product (MVP) to production system.

   b) Key Activities: Highlight key activities and deliverables at each stage.

10. Implement Regular Project Reviews

   a) Review Process: Establish a regular review process to assess progress and realign priorities.

   b) Iterative Improvements: Encourage feedback and continuous improvement.

   c) Outcome Evaluation: Evaluate project outcomes and plan for scaling successful prototypes.

d) Handle Setbacks: Shelve projects with lower ROI without personal attachment, acknowledging the potential for future revisits.

11. Engage with Our Community

   a) Stay Updated: Subscribe to our blog and newsletter for the latest information.

   b) Access Free Resources: Review our free AI glossary regularly to stay familiar with AI terms.

   c) Follow Us: Subscribe to our YouTube channel and follow us on Twitter for more updates.

12. Develop an AI Roadmap

   a) Create a Roadmap: Develop a roadmap based on team insights and discussions.

   b) Identify Projects: Identify short-term and long-term AI projects and allocate resources accordingly.

   c) Follow Our Guide: Use the roadmap provided in our books as a foundation.

13. Conduct a Skills Gap Analysis

   a) Identify Gaps: Determine any skills gaps within the team and plan for necessary training or hiring.

   b) Seek Assistance: Reach out to us or other contractors to fill those gaps.

14. Leverage Subsequent Books and Tools

   a) Continual Learning: Buy a copy of each subsequent book for every team member.

   b) Prototype Implementation: Download and run the free prototype code on an internal server accessible to the team.

c) Evaluate Success: Define success criteria and metrics for evaluation.

15. Maintain Comprehensive Documentation

a) Record Keeping: Keep detailed records of discussions, decisions, and lessons learned throughout the process.

16. Communicate Progress

a) Stakeholder Updates: Regularly update stakeholders on progress and outcomes.

17. Provide Ongoing Support

a) Sustained Success: Ensure that the AI innovation team has ongoing support and resources.

These action items are designed to provide a clear, structured approach for your readers to implement AI innovation within their organizations effectively.

Final Words

As we draw this book to a close, I hope it has served as both a map and a compass in your journey through the evolving landscape of artificial intelligence in business. From understanding the foundational elements of AI to navigating its practical applications and anticipating future trends, our goal has been to prepare you not just to adopt AI but to excel with it.

AI is not merely a technological tool; it is a transformative force that has the potential to redefine the way we work, solve problems, and create value. The journey to integrating AI into your business is challenging, but as we have discussed, it is also replete with opportunities for growth, innovation, and competitive advantage.

Embrace Change: The future belongs to those who are ready to embrace change. AI requires a shift in mindset—from traditional methods of working to more dynamic, data-driven approaches. It demands curiosity, a willingness to experiment, and a readiness to adapt.

Focus on Value Creation: Always align your AI initiatives with the core goal of creating value—whether it's through enhancing efficiency, improving customer satisfaction, or driving revenue growth. AI's true power lies in its ability to transform data into insights and insights into action.

Cultivate Ethical Leadership: As you harness the capabilities of AI, also commit to leading ethically and responsibly. The decisions you make about how AI is used in your business will have lasting impacts not only on your operations but also on your employees, customers, and the wider community.

Stay Informed and Engaged: The field of AI is rapidly advancing. What is innovative today may become standard tomorrow. Continue to learn, stay engaged with the latest developments, and maintain an active dialogue with peers in the field. This ongoing commitment to learning will be crucial to your sustained success.

You Are Not Alone: Remember, you are not alone in this journey. Our community, resources, and expertise are here to support you as you explore, implement, and benefit from AI. We are excited to see how you will apply these ideas to drive your business forward.

Thank you for trusting us as a guide in your AI journey. Hopefully, we inspired you to take bold steps, make informed decisions, and achieve remarkable success in the digital age. Here's to a future where you not only keep pace with AI but lead with it, shaping a world where technology amplifies potential and possibilities are limitless.

Appendices
Resources

Visit our website at AInDotNet.com. If you give us your name and email address and agree to sign up for our free newsletter, we have several free resources for you:

- Cheat Sheet (Glossary) of the top AI terms

- Algorithm Categories

- Directory of AI tools and services

- AI Use Case Evaluation Worksheet

- A newsletter that comes out a few times a month that provides updates on books, coupons, AI humor, AI News, and AI Motivation

For more information:

https://AInDotNet.com

KeithBaldwin@AInDotNet.com

Can You Help Us Spread the Word?

We hope this book has provided you with valuable insights into applying AI to your business, equipping you with the tools and knowledge to confidently begin your AI journey. We designed this book to help you:

- Grasp the essential concepts and terminology of AI.

- Understand AI's transformative potential across various business operations.

- Formulate an effective AI Innovation Team.

- Spot opportunities for integrating AI solutions into your daily processes.

- Navigate the vast array of AI tools and technologies, with a focus on Microsoft platforms.

- Craft a strategic plan for AI adoption that aligns with your business goals and ethical standards.

- Ensure that everyone in your organization—from executives to department managers, project managers, business analysts, programmers, and database administrators—starts from the same baseline and understands the roadmap ahead for developing the most effective AI applications.

- Address many of your AI concerns and questions.

- Guide you through the process of taking a prototype to a minimally viable product, then to a production-ready AI solution, while evaluating ROI at each step.

- Save money, reduce risks, and increase both ROI and functionality using our AI approach.

If these goals resonate with you and you found value in the book, could you please do us a favor? A brief review—where you bought the book—would greatly help us reach more readers and spread the word. Your review doesn't need to be elaborate, just a few sentences can make a huge difference!

Also, please share this book with your coworkers. Ask your boss if you can setup an AI Innovation team.

However, if you feel we missed the mark, or if you have suggestions on how we could improve, we would love to hear from you directly. Your feedback is incredibly important to us as we continue to refine our content. Please send us your thoughts at:

KeithBaldwin@AInDotNet.com

Thank you for your support!

Author Bio

M

y journey in technology began in the early 1970s, starting with building transistor circuits and soon moving on to programming with manual punch cards. By the late 1970s, I was integrating computer systems and peripherals, and in the early 1980s, I explored programming, automation, computer vision, and robotics at the University of Florida (UF). As an undergraduate student, I created and taught college laboratories focused on applying computers and automation to business processes. Computers 40 years ago were as new and novel as AI is today.

During my master's and PhD studies at North Carolina State University (NC State), I discovered my passion for object-oriented programming, artificial intelligence (AI), machine learning (ML), and natural language processing in the mid-1980s. I had graduate studies in statistics, operations research, and other fields that underpin many of today's AI algorithms. At NC State, I also created and taught college labs on applying computers and automation to business processes.

Throughout my career, I've run businesses in manufacturing and laboratory automation and later transitioned to using Microsoft .NET for general IT applications, becoming Microsoft Certified in everything .NET in 2008. I've designed and developed systems across various industries, working closely with subject matter experts (SMEs) and stakeholders and following a thorough design, prototype, minimally viable product and production system.

After getting my kids out of the house (I love my kids but was glad to get them through college and out of the house), I now focus on designing and developing conventional, AI, and ML systems from my barn dominium or cabin, while also enjoying the great outdoors. I live in my own Random Forest. In my spare time, I rescue urban trees from burn piles and landfills to saw into lumber and wood slabs.

My experience spans from the foundational days of computing to the modern era of AI, and I'm excited to share my insights and knowledge in this series of books. I enjoy sharing and applying technical knowledge with others.

AI Images

W

e are writing this book in 2024. A year earlier, Dall-E was bad—very bad. Another AI application called Midjourney was the clear leader in the AI text-to-image market. But Midjourney was difficult to use through Discord and cost an extra $20 per month.

Advancements in AI move very quickly. Dall-E dramatically shrank the gap between Dall-E and Midjourney in only a year, so much so that we decided to use Dall-E for the images in this book.

We want you to see the power of these AI tools. We want you to see some incredible things, such as using AI to generate images and some areas where AI still needs a lot of work.

The point is, that is how most AI is today. AI will often generate four phenomenal things that will leave you stunned and amazed. And then spit out a fifth thing, and you'll think...*What?*

Here's the point of using images that are amazing but contain some obvious flaws:

1. Never leave AI unattended. One of the beauties and drawbacks of AI is that AI is creative, but it's unpredictable.

2. Always log a lot of information about every operation, request, and response.

3. Always ask a human to rate each operation if the results were not as good or better than what the operator could do. Provide a way for the human to provide a note about the operation.

4. Allow anyone on the AI Innovation Team to go through the logs to see what operations AI is doing well and which

operations AI is not doing well. This is the first step to improvement.

5. Do not believe everything that AI tells you. Independently verify, starting with your common sense.

Made in the USA
Columbia, SC
17 February 2025

54007557R00111